D0454093

HEROES OF THE
HOLOCAUST

True Stories of Rescues by Teens

ALLAN ZULLO *and* **MARA BOVSUN**

SCHOLASTIC INC.

NEW YORK   TORONTO   LONDON   AUCKLAND   SYDNEY

MEXICO CITY   NEW DELHI   HONG KONG   BUENOS AIRES

To my good friend Joel Engel,
who makes a difference in everything he does.
—A. Z.

To my father, Jack.
—M. B.

ISBN 0-439-67608-8

12 11 10 9   7 8 9 10/0

Printed in the U.S.A.
First printing, February 2005

www.allanzullo.com

Acknowledgments

We wish to extend our heartfelt gratitude to the persons featured in this book for their willingness to relive, in interviews with us, their emotional, and sometimes painful, memories of their experiences as teenage heroes during World War II.

We also want to thank the following: Stanlee Joyce Stahl, executive vice president, and Bela Spivak, director of allocations, the Jewish Foundation for the Righteous, New York City (**www.jfr.org**); Adaire Klein, director of library and archival services, the Simon Wiesenthal Center, Los Angeles (**www.wiesenthal.com**); Joan Ringelheim, Ph.D., director, department of oral history, Andrew Hollinger, department of media relations, and Steve Luckert, exhibition curator, the United States Holocaust Memorial Museum, Washington, D.C. (**www.ushmm.org**); Carla Lessing, vice president, The Hidden Child Foundation/ADL, New York City (**www.adl.org/hidden**); David G. Marwell, Ph.D., director, The Museum of Jewish Heritage, New York City, (**www.mjhnyc.org**); and the Fortunoff Video Archive for Holocaust Testimonies at Yale University (**www.library.yale.edu/testimonies**).

In addition, we extend a special thank-you to Sonja Munch-Nielsen and Knud Dyby for providing us with vital information about the late Preben Munch-Nielsen.

Authors' Note

You are about to read gripping, true stories of brave young heroes of the Holocaust. These accounts are based exclusively on personal, lengthy interviews conducted with or about each person featured in this book. Using real names, dates, and places, the stories are written as factual and truthful versions of the heroes' recollections, although some of the dialogue has been re-created.

These brave people were not gun-toting, grenade-tossing resistance fighters but rather everyday teenagers who did whatever they could—without weapons—to shield Jews from Nazi savagery. At a time in Europe when so many people looked the other way while innocent victims were being slaughtered, these teens willingly placed their own lives in jeopardy for the sake of saving Jews.

In a ravaged world that had lost its bearings, the heroes in this book were guided by their own moral compasses.

Although the teens came from different backgrounds, countries, and religions, they all shared certain common traits. They acted out of compassion. They showed courage. They were clever. And they believed that one person could make a difference.

It was precisely because this belief was shared by persons of conscience that some victims slipped through the Nazis' web of terror. The young people in this book are typical of countless unheralded heroes who, because of their unshakable values, took action during life-and-death situations to rescue or hide others who were in danger.

Much of what you will read in the following pages might disturb you, but the events really happened. This book is, however, very much a celebration of the goodness in mankind—of the courage of one's convictions and the will to triumph over evil. The stories reveal that in the most horrible situations imaginable, young people possess the guts, faith, and intelligence to aid others, even at great personal risk.

Their harrowing experiences serve as inspiring reminders that only by following our consciences can we prevent another Holocaust.

Allan Zullo and
Mara Bovsun

Contents

———◆◆◆———

MAP OF EUROPE 1939–1945

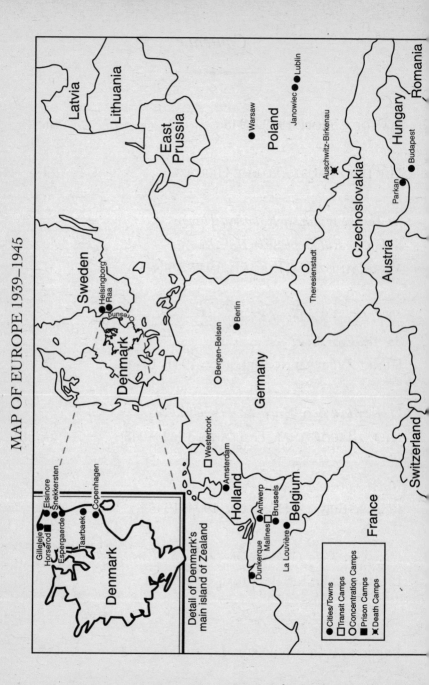

Detail of Denmark's main island of Zealand

Legend:
- ● Cities/Towns
- □ Transit Camps
- ○ Concentration Camps
- ■ Prison Camps
- ✖ Death Camps

The Holocaust and the Heroes

Led by dictator Adolf Hitler, the Nazi Party in Germany in the 1930s and 1940s believed that certain people — particularly Jews, Gypsies, homosexuals, and the disabled — were inferior and didn't deserve to live.

The Nazis were anti-Semitic, which means they hated Jewish people. Although many Jews were doctors, lawyers, businessmen, bankers, and teachers who contributed a great deal to German society, Hitler blamed them for the country's economic problems. The truth was that Germany was going through a difficult time because it had been badly defeated in World War I, which ended in 1918.

Hitler and his parliament passed laws that required Jews to give up their jobs, their homes, their businesses, and their rights. To enforce these laws, the police organization known as the Gestapo and an elite army corps known as the SS imprisoned, beat, and murdered Jews — simply because they were Jewish. Non-Jews who opposed the Nazis' authority suffered similar treatment. Many Jews and political enemies of the Nazis were sent to brutal prisons known as concentration camps.

Hitler was determined to protect at all costs "German blood and German honor" for the country's Aryans, the name given to white, non-Jewish Germans. He was also determined to invade and occupy *all* of Europe.

In March 1938, Germany took over Austria and put into effect harsh new laws that stripped Austrian Jews of their rights. Then, in September 1939, German troops invaded Poland. This caused Great Britain and France, who were allies of Poland, to declare war on Germany, thus triggering the start of World War II. The following year, Nazi forces invaded and occupied Denmark, Norway, Belgium, Holland, and Luxembourg. Then France fell, and Great Britain was battered by German air assaults. In December 1941, the United States entered the war and joined the Soviet Union (which included Russia), Great Britain, and the Free French (an organization fighting for the liberation of France) to form the Allied Forces, which were determined to halt the German war machine.

As country after country fell under Nazi occupation, Jews were singled out for mistreatment, just as they were in Germany. They had to wear the six-pointed Star of David, a symbol of Judaism, on their sleeves, chests, or backs to tell them apart from non-Jews. They couldn't walk freely in the streets or do many of the things Europeans took for granted. Signs in theaters, cafés, restaurants, and other public places warned that Jews weren't allowed to enter.

During the war years, the Nazis created ghettos. These were small areas inside cities, usually several blocks, that were sealed by brick or stone walls or barbed wire where Jews were forced to live under unhealthy and crowded conditions. Every month, tens of thousands of Jews were deported: They were moved from ghettos to forced-labor or concentration camps where, unless they were useful to the Nazis, they were killed in gas chambers or murdered in some other way. It was all part of Hitler's "Final Solution," the Nazi plan to eliminate all the Jews of Europe.

As the war came to an end in 1945, the Allies liberated the imprisoned Jews, although hundreds of thousands were barely alive because of Nazi cruelty. The world was shocked to discover that of the 9 million Jews who lived in Europe before the war, 6 million had been murdered or had died from starvation or disease in Nazi camps. Of the Jewish children who failed to escape from Europe after 1939, more than 1.5 million were murdered by the Nazis or were deported to camps where they died of illness or hunger. Another 4 million civilians, including 3 million Polish Catholics, died at the hands of the Nazis.

This horrific mass murder is called the Holocaust, a word from ancient Greece meaning "sacrifice by fire." Over time, the word came to mean the slaughter of a large number of human beings.

The cruelty went virtually unchecked because, out of fear, anti-Semitism, or self-protection, millions of non-Jewish Europeans couldn't or wouldn't get involved in stopping the Nazi madness. It's estimated that only one half of one percent of European non-Jews tried to help Jews. Sadly, many Europeans actively supported the Nazis by turning in Jews and those who assisted Jews. These morally bankrupt people were known as collaborators, informants, or Nazi sympathizers.

Yet thousands of victims survived the Holocaust thanks to people who were willing to risk their lives to save others. These heroes came from all walks of life. They were rich and poor, young and old, and from every war-torn country.

When it was more practical to remain quiet and not get involved, when it was safer to go into hiding, these heroes dared to outsmart the Nazis, knowing that if caught, they faced arrest, deportation to a concentration camp, or immediate execution.

In big and small ways, these brave citizens came to the aid of the persecuted. Some were members of secret groups known as the underground or the Resistance, or were partisans who sabotaged the German army and helped Jews escape the Nazis. Other heroes quietly fed or hid Jews (sometimes for years) or smuggled them to safety. And there were those who provided fake identity cards, birth certificates, visas, and work permits to prevent Jews from falling into the clutches of the enemy.

For more than forty years, Yad Vashem, an organization that creates Holocaust museums, exhibits, archives, and monuments in Jerusalem, has been honoring what it calls the Righteous Among the Nations, non-Jews who risked their lives to save Jews. To date, more than 20,000 such heroes have been recognized, including family members who helped in the rescues. Each person recognized as a Righteous Among the Nations has been awarded a specially minted medal inscribed with a passage from the Talmud, a holy collection of Jewish laws and traditions. It says: "Whoever saves a single life has saved the entire world." The hero also receives a certificate of honor and has his or her name added to the Wall of Honor in the Garden of the Righteous Among the Nations in Jerusalem.

The Holocaust will remain a sacred and painful memory of the millions who perished. Yet in the darkest hours of the human race, the lights of compassion and courage still glowed, thanks to the heroes of the Holocaust.

"If They're Willing to Kill Jews, They're Willing to Kill People Who Hide Jews"

MARIA ANDZELM, POLAND, 1942–1944

Her heart breaking, Maria "Marysia" Andzelm gazed into the sad eyes of her best friend, Rivka Rubinowicz, and sighed. "I'll miss you so much."

"Good-bye, Marysia," Rivka blurted in a voice cracking in anguish. "We'll never see each other again."

"Don't say that," Maria said, wiping away her own tears. "You'll be back once the war is over. Then we'll be friends again. You'll see."

After a final hug, Rivka stepped away and shook her head. "No, I won't be coming back."

Deep down inside, as she watched her friend trudge off, Maria knew Rivka was right.

Rivka was a Jew in Nazi-occupied Poland. For months, the Nazis had been rounding up Jews and taking them away, never to be seen again. Now, on this otherwise beautiful spring day in May 1942, the

120 Jewish families of the little Polish town of Janowiec were facing immediate deportation.

No one knew where they were going, but they all had heard the horrible stories about how Jewish children just like Rivka and her parents — tens of thousands of them — were shoved into trucks and trains like animals and taken away.

Maria, a Catholic, couldn't understand why the Jews were so hated. *I wish there was something I could do to help them,* thought the petite thirteen-year-old farm girl. *I feel so helpless, so sad.*

Rivka and Maria had been friends for about four years. They spent much of their time together sewing dolls, hiking in the nearby pine forests, and swimming in the Vistula, the wide river that flowed next to their town. During every Passover — the Jewish holiday celebrating the Hebrews' liberation from slavery — Rivka would bring Maria a piece of matzo, flat bread eaten at the ceremonial dinner.

The two girls often talked about their dreams for the future. They wanted to someday live in a big city and have a life far different from what most young women in Janowiec faced — being a farmer's wife. Maria had been to a big city just once — Warsaw, about seventy-five miles away — but she had barely caught a glimpse of it. As luck would have it, Maria and her family arrived in Warsaw on September 1, 1939, the very day the Nazis invaded Poland. The Andzelms had turned right around and rushed home.

None of Maria's other friends would play with Rivka, and although they would never say why, Maria knew the reason. It was because Rivka was Jewish.

"Why should it matter what her religion is?" Maria asked her parents, Stefan and Valeria.

"It doesn't matter, Marysia," her father said. "She is your friend, that's what's important." Maria liked the way her father could make things seem so clear, especially when it came to right and wrong. He didn't have to remind her that judging people by their religion was very wrong.

But few of the Andzelms' neighbors felt the same way after the Nazis roared into town and set up their local headquarters in a nearby hilltop castle, the oldest and largest in Poland.

At first, life went on as usual for the Andzelms. Maria, her younger brothers, Stanislaw and Jan, her parents, and her grandmother Josepha (called *Babcia*, Polish for Grandma) worked the family farm on the edge of town. But there were constant and sometimes painful reminders that they lived in a country occupied by the Nazis, who often took what they wanted from the Poles, including food, livestock, and even family heirlooms.

Once, after the Nazis made the family give up one of its two cows, Maria heard her mother complain bitterly to Stefan. "We barely have enough for ourselves," Valeria said. "We can't keep giving the Germans anything they want. We're poor. Why, the children don't even have shoes."

"We have no choice," Stefan replied. "One does not argue with the Nazis. If we don't give them what they want, they'll take it anyway and make life worse for us."

Maria knew that was true — and it made her feel helpless.

In early 1942, Maria and her family heard frightening news that had filtered in from other parts of Poland, nightmarish stories about Jews being torn from their homes, driven into the woods, and shot . . . of terrible places called concentration camps, where Jews were starved, worked to death, or murdered.

The stories were so awful that Maria at first didn't believe her ears. But then she began seeing the Nazi horror firsthand. It started when all the Jews from a town across the Vistula were brought to Janowiec and forced to clean the streets on their hands and knees. She saw formerly well-to-do shop owners, schoolteachers, and businessmen now looking like beggars. They were ragged, starving, and terrified, yet none of the townspeople could help them; the Nazis warned of dire consequences for anyone who tried.

One night, there was a knock on the Andzelms' door. When Maria and her grandmother answered it, they reeled from the pitiful sight in front of them. Outside stood a young woman in a tattered coat, clutching what looked like a bundle of rags in her arms.

"Please, some milk for my baby," the woman begged.

"Marysia," *Babcia* said. "Go get some milk and a piece of bread. Hurry!"

When Maria handed her the food, the woman murmured a thank-you and disappeared into the night.

The woman returned several times, as did other walking skeletons, all asking for food. They were Jews who had fled from other parts of Poland where the Germans had taken over. Now they were on the run, hiding in the woods, praying that they could stay one step ahead of the Nazis.

The size of the meals at the Andzelm house got smaller as more Jews showed up at the door pleading for something to eat. Valeria couldn't buy more food because it would raise suspicions from Nazis or collaborators that she was feeding more than just the members of her family. To feed a Jew could cost a person his life.

"I'm still hungry," seven-year-old Jan complained after a meager dinner. He started to cry. "Why do we have to give our food away?"

"Because what we have, we share," Stefan explained in a voice that made it clear he expected no argument. "As the Golden Rule says, 'Do to others as you would have them do to you.'"

The Andzelms continued to give some of their food to the Jewish refugees until no more came to the door. The Nazis had deported all the Jews in Janowiec, including Rivka and her parents. Where they went, no one knew for sure.

A few months later, the Andzelms had a visitor late at night. It was Mr. Milosz, an old friend from town. Maria was in bed, but she could hear him say, "Stefan, we need your help." The two men started talking in a whisper, and Maria couldn't make out what they were saying. She soon drifted off to sleep.

The next day, Stefan called Maria, Jan, and

Stanislaw into the back room of their house. "We must keep a very important secret," he said softly. "We're going to take in two Jewish men."

Maria and her brothers said nothing.

"We're going to hide them from the Nazis," Stefan continued. "Don't say anything to anybody, because if you do, you know what will happen, right?"

"Yes, Papa," said Stanislaw, who had just turned ten. "If we get caught, we'll all be killed."

Everyone was aware of the penalty for hiding Jews, although no one had been caught yet in Janowiec. But the Andzelm children had heard reports that in other Polish cities — Warsaw, Krakow, and Lublin — non-Jews had paid the ultimate price for trying to help a Jewish friend or save a Jewish child. Some were shot. Others were hanged in the street, left dangling with a sign that said, FOR HIDING A JEW.

"If you keep quiet about this, then our Jewish guests will remain alive and we will, too," Stefan told his children. "These men deserve to live, just like we do."

Maria felt mixed emotions — anxiety that she would be caught helping Jews and satisfaction in trying to save them. Although worried that she and the rest of the family were putting their own lives on the line, Maria was convinced it was worth the risk. *What if I were Jewish?* she wondered. *Wouldn't I want someone to help me?*

The next morning, she learned from her father that the two Jewish men had arrived during the night and were staying in a shed behind the house where her uncle, Miezyslaw Chechulski, a shoemaker, lived with his wife and two daughters.

"The Jewish men are now hiding where Uncle Miezyslaw stores his potatoes," Stefan told Maria. "They have to stay there until Mr. Milosz, your uncle, and I prepare a hideout in our barn. We have to dig a big hole and build an underground box for them to live in. It'll take a few days, and we mustn't be seen by anyone. You're going to have to look out for Germans and nosy neighbors while we dig. Remember, a lot of people would turn us in for helping these Jews."

For two nights, Stefan, Mr. Milosz, and Uncle Miezyslaw worked in the barn, digging, hammering, and sawing while Maria and her brothers watched for the Gestapo or any suspicious neighbors.

Maria jumped every time one of the men hit a nail. *What if the Nazis hear the hammering?* she asked herself. *What if they see the boards being brought into the barn? What if they see Uncle Miezyslaw moving the dirt from the barn?*

On the first night, Maria and her mother brought bowls of potato soup to the two Jews in the small potato shack. Maria recognized one of the men. He was the barber, Srulik Schwarzfort, the thirty-six-year-old son of Janowiec's *felczer*, or doctor. Many times Srulik and his father would rush out at night when someone was sick or hurt. It didn't matter to them if patients couldn't pay or weren't Jewish. "If you have money, you pay. If not, that's okay," the *felczer* would say to each patient. "You're my neighbor, so you're like family."

Maria had never seen the other man before. She noticed that he was much younger than Srulik and was tall and had curly brown hair. Like Srulik, he was wearing dirty clothes from spending several days hiding in the woods. He looked at her with weary eyes. *If he were cleaned up and not being hunted, he could be pretty cute,* thought Maria. Then she scolded herself. *Oh, you stupid girl. How could you even have such a thought?*

"Thank you," the young man said when Maria handed him the bowl. She nodded and, without uttering a word, walked away.

The next evening when Maria brought them their dinner, the younger man again thanked her and said, "I'm Moses Kershenbaum."

"Maria," she replied shyly before returning to the house.

Moments later, she heard a great commotion outside. When she looked through the window, she saw two Polish police officers dragging Jakob Poznanski, the eighteen-year-old son of the town butcher. Jakob was a Jew. Following behind were dozens of townspeople, some yelling, some waving their fists. They were heading toward the nearby cemetery.

"*Babcia*, what're they doing with Jakob?" Maria asked her grandmother.

Babcia peered outside and then shook her head. "Get away from the window, Marysia," she ordered.

Suddenly, they heard *bam, bam, bam*.

Soon the crowd walked away from the cemetery and past the Andzelms' house. Maria peeked out the window and saw people laughing and joking. She couldn't make out what they were saying until a voice rose above the racket: "That was one tough Jew. It took three bullets to kill him."

Maria sank to the floor and covered her mouth in shock. *Oh, my God! They killed the poor boy in cold blood! How could they do such a horrible thing? Because he was a*

Jew? What would those awful people do if they knew two more Jews were hiding so close to them? Maria shuddered at the thought.

Later that night, Mr. Milosz came over and told the Andzelms what had happened. "When the Nazis rounded up the Jews in town, Jakob slipped into the woods and hid. After a while, he went back to his house to get a suit that he had left there. He wanted to sell it to get money for food. One of his neighbors, Lech Belka, followed him into the house and warned him that the police were coming. He persuaded Jakob to go into the cellar and hide from them. But it was a trick. Belka locked the cellar door and ran to the Gestapo. He was hoping to get a reward for turning in a Jew, maybe get an extra ration of bread or sugar.

"When Belka announced he had trapped a Jew, the Gestapo said they had enough to do without coming out to kill one Jewish teenager. They told him to do it himself. So a crowd from town went out to watch him shoot a Jew."

"There are people in our own town who'll murder an innocent boy just for an extra ration of bread or sugar?" Maria said in disbelief.

Mr. Milosz nodded.

"It's sickening, shocking," Stefan declared.

"Jakob was born here, grew up here before their very eyes. He was a nice boy. This shouldn't be happening here."

Maria felt sick to her stomach. *It's one thing to have Nazis killing Jews, but to have my own neighbors doing it, too? Why, these are the same people I see in church. This is madness!* She suddenly felt extremely afraid. *My God, that means we're surrounded by murderers. And if they're willing to kill Jews, they're willing to kill people who hide Jews.*

It had taken only two days for the hideout to be built, but it seemed so much longer to Maria because she was afraid someone would squeal on them to the Gestapo. The hiding place was a box under the floor of the barn in the pen where the cows stayed. It had a small hatch at the top with a hinge made of leather straps. On top of the box the men spread a thick layer of manure and straw. Even up close, no one would see that the floor of the barn had been disturbed. No one would guess that there were two men hunched underneath it.

Like a grave, Maria thought when the men jumped into the hideout. *Like a grave for the living.*

A week later, the men crept out of the hiding place at night and hurried into the house, where they washed up and talked to the family. Maria couldn't help but notice that the men smelled of cow manure and urine.

"It all leaks through the top of the box and onto our heads," said Moses.

Even after they cleaned up, both men were still uncomfortable. They were scratching itchy red marks on their skin. "Fleas," Moses explained. "The straw in our hideout is infested with them. They're eating us alive, but it's better than trying to survive in the woods."

With Maria listening intently, Moses told the family about himself. He had come from a nearby town where he lived with his mother and two brothers. His father had died ten years earlier, and his older sister had married and gone to France before the war. When the Germans invaded Poland, Moses joined the Polish army, but it quickly disbanded, leaving him stranded. He hiked back home, moving quickly and quietly at night in the woods because the countryside was crawling with German soldiers.

When he arrived home, he was relieved to see that his mother and brothers were alive. But his joy was short-lived. Soon the Germans issued orders that all Jews were to be taken away.

On the night before the deportations, his mother walked with him to the banks of the Vistula River and handed him five gold pieces. "Moses, your brothers have families of their own and won't leave them," she said. "You're single. You have a chance. This is all the money we have. Take it and go find a place to hide. Maybe you, of all of us, will survive."

Moses found a boat and rowed across the Vistula to Janowiec, where he knew a few people, including Srulik, who also decided to go into hiding rather than be deported. Srulik enlisted the help of Mr. Milosz. He found them a place to hide, but they soon were forced to leave because the people who agreed to conceal them became frightened. Twice more, the two men had to leave hiding places in homes because the owners suddenly demanded an unreasonable amount of money or were acting suspiciously.

Finally, Mr. Milosz brought them to Stefan, who agreed to hide them in his barn. Stefan asked for no money, nothing in return, even though he was putting his entire family in peril. "It's the only thing to do because it's the right thing to do," he told Maria.

For months the two men stayed in the hideout, coming out at night or when they were certain no one would see them. The fleas continued to bite, even when new straw was put down, and manure and urine kept leaking in. Worst of all was the boredom.

"If we could just have something to read, a book, anything," Moses said to Maria.

"Our neighbor, Mrs. Olejarczyk, has books," Maria said. "She has a whole wall of them."

"Do you think she'd let you borrow one?"

"I'll go ask."

The next day, Maria visited Mrs. Olejarczyk and asked if she could see her books.

"Of course, Maria," replied the woman, guiding her into the living room.

Maria looked at the unfamiliar names and titles on the leather spines of books crammed on rows of shelves.

"Why are you so interested in my books?" Mrs. Olejarczyk asked.

"The books in school are so boring, and I was hoping I could borrow one from you."

"I didn't know you were such a big reader."

"I'm not, but I want to find something that will take my mind off the war." Maria pulled out *Satirical Poems* by Siegfried Sassoon. "Is this any good?"

Mrs. Olejarczyk shook her head and frowned. "You wouldn't like it. Besides, he's a Jew." She took the book from Maria and threw it on the floor. "I shouldn't even have it in my house." Then she selected another book and handed it to Maria. It was

The Hunchback of Notre Dame by a French author, Victor Hugo. "Have you read this one?"

"No, but I'd like to. I've heard a lot about it."

"Then take it home and return it to me when you're finished."

"Oh, thank you, Mrs. Olejarczyk," Maria said.

That night, after Maria had taken food to the two men, she slipped the book down into the hideout, which was lit by a tiny kerosene lamp. Moses flashed her a big smile and said, "Like food for the stomach, this is food for the mind. I am so grateful to you, Maria."

She blushed and hurried back to the house. The next week, she returned the book to Mrs. Olejarczyk.

"Back so soon?" asked Mrs. Olejarczyk. "My, you must be a fast reader. How did you like it?"

"Oh, it was wonderful," said Maria, who hadn't read the novel.

"What was your favorite part?"

Uh-oh, she thought. *This could be big trouble. Stay calm. You know just enough about it that maybe you can bluff her.* "I liked when the beautiful Gypsy girl helped out the hunchback." She immediately grabbed another book off the shelf without even looking at the title and said, "May I borrow this one?"

"The History of the French Revolution? That's an odd choice for a young girl. But if you want to . . . "

"Oh, thank you. I have to hurry back and tend to the cows. Bye." As she left the house with the new book, Maria realized that to keep Mrs. Olejarczyk from getting suspicious, she would have to read — and learn — something from each book she took. *If I can tell her a few things about the book, then she'll believe I've read it.*

Week after week, Maria borrowed from Mrs. Olejarczyk's personal library novels, classics, poetry, and books on all kinds of subjects, including works meant for university scholars, not a teenage farm girl. Yet every time Maria was questioned, she was prepared. She even went so far as to memorize complete passages.

Because her parents worked the farm by themselves, Maria was responsible for feeding Srulik and Moses and bringing them books. While Stanislaw watched for Nazis and neighbors, Maria carried food out to the barn three times a day. It took her six trips because she could carry only one dish at a time. This routine continued for two years, and with each passing day, Maria wondered when their luck — and hers — would run out.

She was most fearful whenever she saw her little

brother Jan playing with his friends. *What if he makes one little slip of the tongue and someone learns about our family secret? Can Jan keep a secret? For that matter, can Stanislaw? Can I? One wrong word to the wrong person can mean death for all of us. And what will I say if a Nazi catches me carrying soup out to the barn? If I act at all afraid, he'll know we're hiding Jews.*

As if Maria and her family didn't have enough to worry about, black-booted German soldiers would come into the town unannounced at night and snatch older children from their beds — it didn't matter that they were Christian — and take them to Germany to work for the Nazi war effort.

Usually Maria's father and Mr. Milosz knew through the underground when these surprise sweeps would happen. Whenever they were alerted, Maria and other young people would hide in the caves of nearby quarries and sit there all night until someone came to tell them it was safe to return home.

But sometimes there wasn't enough time to flee, and Maria and her family had to resort to trickery.

"Marysia, get into bed right now!" Stefan ordered one day. "The Nazis are here!"

Maria dashed into her room, threw off her dress, and dived into bed. Rushing in right behind her, Valeria hurriedly rubbed red crepe paper on Maria's cheeks to make it look as if she had a fever. Then Valeria plopped a bottle of medicine on the bedside table to complete the impression that Maria was sick.

Seconds later, two soldiers burst into the room. "We've come for your daughter," said one of the Nazis. "She's needed for the war effort."

"As you can see, she's very sick," said Valeria. "A bad fever and cough."

Between moans, Maria began hacking and breathing hard.

Then Valeria started coughing. "It's contagious. I think I'm getting it, too."

The soldiers looked at each other and backed out of the room. They never returned. But every now and then, they would look for young people in the village.

One day, after borrowing another book from Mrs. Olejarczyk, Maria was walking along the road daydreaming. She didn't realize until it was too late that a German officer was approaching her. *Oh, my God, he's going to take me away,* she thought.

"*Sprechen sie Deutsch?*" the officer asked. ("Do you speak German?")

Maria had learned some German in school, but

not enough to carry on a conversation, especially when she was petrified. Besides, many Poles refused to speak German even if they knew the language, just to annoy the Nazis.

"*Nein,*" she sputtered out. ("No.")

The officer glared at her, his blue eyes blazing. Then he slapped her hard across the face and stormed off.

Her cheek stung, but she still felt relief — he hadn't taken her away. From then on, Maria became extra careful whenever she walked to or from Mrs. Olejarczyk's house.

One morning in May, almost two years since Srulik and Moses had begun hiding in the barn, Maria woke up to violent knocking at the door. Her parents were out in the field. Only her grandmother and brothers were in the house. *Babcia* opened the door and came face-to-face with a Nazi officer.

"All the adults must line up at the church at noon," he barked. "We have to see who's here. Do you understand, old woman?"

Babcia nodded, and the officer stomped off. Moments later, after the officer was out of sight, Maria's parents returned to the house. "We just heard from Mr. Milosz that the Nazis have surrounded the town," Stefan said. "This is a bad sign. They're looking for people they suspect of being members of the underground. The Nazis won't do anything to *Babcia*, so she can go. But we have to hide."

"I'll help you," said Maria.

She followed her parents as they hustled out to the barn and opened the lid to the hideout. "You've got company," Stefan told the two surprised men. He lowered his wife into the box and then jumped down. "Maria, take the pitchfork and cover the hideout with straw," Stefan ordered from below. "Hurry."

Once the lid was closed, Maria quickly spread hay over it. She was putting the pitchfork away when she was startled to see a Nazi officer standing in the barn. *Oh, no! How long has he been here? Did he see me covering up the hideout? What's he going to say? What's he going to do? Be ready for anything. If he knows people are down there, he'll kill them . . . and me, too. But not without fighting me first.* She clutched the pitchfork in her hand. When the officer moved closer to her, Maria was so scared she thought she would pass out. She recognized him as the Nazi who had come to the door earlier that morning.

"Where are your parents?" he demanded.

For several seconds Maria couldn't speak. Her mouth was dry from fear. Then she found her voice.

"They went to the church like you ordered," Maria lied, looking him right in the eyes. "My grandmother, too."

The German grunted and walked away. With shaking knees, she ran to the house and collapsed on her bed.

Babcia returned from the church late in the afternoon. She had been crying.

"*Babcia*, what happened?" asked Maria.

"They made us gather outside the church and the Nazis started pulling men out of line, dozens of them, and then they took them away. Maria, the Nazis aren't after only the Jews anymore. They're after the Poles, too."

Not until later in the evening, after her parents had returned to the house, did Maria and her family learn from Mr. Milosz how horrific the day was for the people of Janowiec. "Thanks to some despicable informers, the Nazis rounded up sixty-three men and took them out of town and forced them to dig a big hole," he reported. "Then the men were ordered to kneel in front of the hole, and one by one, they were all shot. They fell into the mass grave that they had just dug."

Sickened by the awful news, Maria closed her eyes, wrapped her arms around herself, and doubled over. "When will the killing stop?" she cried. "When will this war be over?"

"Soon," Mr. Milosz replied. "It's only a matter of months now. All the news from the underground says the Russians are advancing and the Germans are growing weaker and more desperate each day. By fall, the war will be over. You'll see."

For the people of Janowiec, the war ended sooner than expected — but not without tragedy.

On August 2, 1944, Maria went to town to visit a friend, Leah Mazur, who lived a few doors away from Maria's aunt Hella. Suddenly, their conversation was interrupted by a burst of gunfire followed by explosions from bombs dropped by Soviet planes. The girls found themselves caught in the crossfire of a raging battle between the advancing Russian army and the retreating German forces.

Dodging bullets, Maria and Leah dashed to Aunt Hella's barn, which had a cellar that offered some protection. They joined two dozen other townspeople who were already huddling there. For hours and hours, the loud noise of the fierce fighting was unbearable. Shrapnel clattered against the barn's tin roof like metal hail, blasts from nearby bombs shook the earth, and grenades rattled the ears of those trapped in the cellar. Machine-gun fire drowned out the shouts and moans of dying and wounded soldiers.

What bothered Maria the most wasn't the concern over being killed by a bomb or a grenade; there was nothing she could do about that. She was racked with anxiety over not knowing the fate of her parents, brothers, and grandmother. She wondered, *Are they safe? Are they in the hideout? Were they somewhere else when the battle broke out? And what about Srulik and Moses? They've been hiding for more than two years. They can't die now.*

Maria and the others remained in the cellar for several days until the barrage finally eased. During a lull in the shooting, one boy stood up and announced, "I want to see what's going on. I need to find my father."

"No, don't go out there!" shouted the others. "It's not safe!" But he refused to listen to them and bolted out of the cellar.

Less than an hour later, the boy burst into the cellar, crying hysterically. "My father is dead!" he screamed. "And so is Mr. Andzelm!"

Hearing her father's name, Maria shrieked and ran for the door. "Papa! Papa!" she wailed.

"Marysia, calm down," ordered her aunt, grabbing her. "It can't be your father. It's probably the other Mr. Andzelm."

As much as Maria wanted to believe that, she knew better. "The other Mr. Andzelm lives far across town," she blurted. "He never comes this way." She started kicking and struggling to get away. "That was my father. I know. Let me go!"

"No, Marysia, you can't go!" Aunt Hella said. "There's nothing you can do for him." She held Maria tightly until the frantic girl stopped fighting and fell into a heap at her feet.

The next day, a Russian soldier entered the cellar. "You have to leave here," he said. "The whole town is being evacuated. You must get to the other side of the Vistula, where it's now controlled by the Soviet army. You'll be safer there. Go as fast as you can."

"There are still planes overhead dropping bombs, and soldiers are still shooting," Aunt Hella protested. "We'll be out in the open. We'll be killed."

"You must get out of here and go to the other side of the river," the Russian replied. "You have no choice. Now go, all of you!"

Everyone streamed out of the cellar and managed to make it safely to the river. There, Maria found her mother, brothers, and grandmother, but she sensed the tears they were shedding weren't all out of happiness at seeing her.

"Where's Papa?" Maria asked. "Oh, Mama, please don't tell me . . ."

Valeria hugged Maria and wept. Maria's legs went weak and she sobbed, "Oh, Papa, Papa."

"Your father died while saving Moses and Srulik," said Valeria. "When we were ordered by the Russians to get to the other side of the river, we all started running. Papa went to the barn to tell Moses and Srulik that they needed to leave. When they came out, they were spotted by that horrible neighbor, Gorski. He was with a policeman, and he started shouting, 'I knew it! I knew it! Andzelm was hiding Jews! Arrest him!' The policeman pulled out his gun and shot Papa. Moses and Srulik escaped, and so did we."

"We saw it all," said Stanislaw. Then a grim smile crossed his lips. "At least Gorski and the policeman got what they deserved. Right after Papa was shot, an artillery shell exploded next to them and killed them both."

"Marysia, take Jan and *Babcia* and go with Aunt Hella to the other side," Valeria said. "Keep walking east, and look for a farmer who'll take you in. We'll find you later. Stanislaw, come with me."

"Mama, where are you and Stanislaw going?" Maria asked.

"We have to bury your father."

After Valeria and Stanislaw headed back to the house, the rest of the family found a man who agreed to take them across the river in his rowboat. But gunfire erupted again during the crossing. Although they were easy targets for the Germans and faced death or injury from a stray bullet or shrapnel, Maria was no longer scared. All she could think about was that she'd never see her father again.

They reached the other side safely and ran into the forest, but it was clear from the battle that they needed to go farther away from the river. They hiked until they reached a ramshackle house on a farm that had been neglected. A weary woman answered the door and invited them to stay. She told them her name was Paulina Augustyn and that her husband had gone off to war, leaving her alone. She did the best she could, but the farm was too much to tend by herself.

A few days later, Valeria and Stanislaw arrived. It was a bittersweet reunion.

"We found Papa's body," Stanislaw told Maria. "We put him in a wooden coffin and dragged it to the cemetery. We had no time to dig a grave because another battle started right near us. So we pushed his coffin into a bomb crater and covered it as best we could. Papa deserved so much better."

"The farm was destroyed," said Valeria. "The animals were either killed or stolen. There's no reason ever to go back to Janowiec, even though we have family there."

"Why don't you stay here?" Paulina suggested. "With my husband gone, I need help working the farm. I can't do it alone."

The family accepted her invitation. When the Nazis finally were pushed out of the region days later, Aunt Hella and *Babcia* returned to Janowiec. Maria and her mother and brothers remained with Paulina. They helped get the farm back in shape and cut wheat and rye from sunrise to sunset. It was hard, painful, boring work. Maria had nothing to cover her bare legs, and the hard ends of the straw cut into her skin. Day after day, she worked without complaining, but in her heart she was always weeping.

What will become of me? she wondered. Her dreams of a better life in a big city grew dimmer. *There is nothing in my future.*

But then, in September, a Polish soldier came to the farm and said that he had a message from a man in Lublin, Moses Kershenbaum. "He wants all of you to join him," the soldier said. "He'd have come himself, but these parts are still too dangerous for a Jew alone."

"He's alive and well?" Maria asked.

"Yes," the soldier answered. "He said that when fighting broke out in Janowiec he and his friend escaped to Lublin. Moses took any work he could get. As soon as he had a room, some food, and money, he devoted all his energy to finding the people who had saved him. Your relatives in Janowiec told him where you were living."

Maria was deeply touched by Moses' gesture. *Our family has paid a terrible price for hiding him and now he's trying to repay his debt,* she thought. *What a good-hearted, decent man.*

Valeria, Stanislaw, and Jan left for Lublin while Maria stayed behind to help Paulina with the fall harvest. Then, on a bitterly cold day in November 1944, a horse-drawn cart came for Maria to take her to her family. With the temperature below freezing, she choose to go on foot most of the twenty-five miles to Lublin, hoping the body heat generated by walking would help keep her warm.

She was tired and her fingers and toes were numb, but for some reason that she couldn't fully understand, Maria felt happy. *Papa always said that if you do something good, something good will happen to you. Maybe there is a bright future for me after all.* Maria smiled and kept on walking, each step taking her farther away from the past and closer to a new life.

Maria joined her mother and brothers in Lublin, where they lived in a room paid for by Moses. He found Maria a job and they became good friends. They eventually fell in love, and on October 25, 1945, Maria, who was only sixteen, married Moses.

Believing there was nothing for them in Poland, the couple came to the United States in 1949 with their first baby. They eventually settled in Red Bank, New Jersey, where they operated a cigar store and raised two daughters, Rosalie and Helene. Moses and Maria remained a loving couple for fifty-two years until he died of heart disease in 1997 at the age of eighty-three.

Maria's mother, brothers, and grandmother chose to stay in Poland. Srulik Schwarzfort, who had escaped with Moses, immigrated to Israel.

Of all the Jews in Janowiec, only two survived — the two who were hidden by the Andzelm family.

Years later, when asked why he thought the family willingly defied the Nazis at their own peril to save his life,

Moses replied, "They are angels. You seldom find people like that."

In 1994, Maria Kershenbaum was honored by Yad Vashem as one of the Righteous Among the Nations. Her name is inscribed on the Wall of Honor next to the names of her late mother and father.

"Will I Ever See Any of You Again? Are You Even Alive?"

HENRI ZYLBERMINC, BELGIUM, 1941–1944

Henri Zylberminc sensed something was wrong the moment Gerhard Spaak, a fellow student, walked into the classroom wearing the black uniform of a Belgian Nazi.

It had been unsettling times for Jews like Henri ever since Germany had invaded Belgium the previous year, in May 1940. Within months, the Germans had adopted the first of many anti-Jewish laws and ordinances. They banned certain Jewish religious practices, restricted the civil rights of Jews, and forbade Jews from teaching and practicing law and medicine. But sixteen-year-old Henri had yet to experience any anti-Semitism at his school, the Royal Athenaeum, in Brussels. In school, he studied hard, sang in student theatrical productions, and had an outgoing personality that made him popular. The classroom was his refuge from the growing Nazi menace in the outside world.

"Why are you wearing that awful uniform?" Henri asked Gerhard, who had been seated next to him in class since the fall term began, in 1941.

"You don't have to worry," replied Gerhard. "Nothing is going to happen to you." Then he flashed a sinister grin and added, "Yet."

The next day, Henri and his brothers, Jack, fourteen, and Paul, nine, were about to enter the school when Gerhard blocked their path. "You can't come to school anymore," he said.

"Quit joking around, Gerhard, and get out of our way," growled Henri.

But Gerhard didn't budge. Instead, he pointed to a sign on the front door and told them, "It's from the SS Command of Jewish Affairs." In big, bold black letters, the sign read: "All Jews are banned from attending any public school in Belgium. Any Jewish student who is caught in class or any teacher who knowingly allows a Jew to attend class will face severe punishment."

The words hit Henri like a sucker punch to the gut. *Not attend school anymore? Is this a sick joke? This can't really be true, can it?* He looked up and saw his teacher standing in the doorway. His expression — one of sadness and helplessness — convinced Henri that this ban was all too real.

When the Zylberminc brothers returned home, Henri flung his books onto the floor. "Do you believe this?" he ranted. "Why are the Nazis picking on us? What did we ever do to them?"

His parents, Abram and Minka, tried to settle him down.

"It's not just Jewish children the Nazis are hurting," said Abram. "This is part of the latest Nazi proclamation. Jews can't own businesses or work for the city, and the Nazis are taking Jewish property and shops."

"What are you going to do?" Henri asked.

"We'll go on working as we have since the war began," replied Abram. "We'll just do it quietly, so the Nazis don't know."

Henri's parents owned a business that made custom-tailored clothes for the wealthy of Brussels. It was on the ground floor of their two-story house in Laeken, a fashionable suburb with few Jewish families but many prominent people and royalty, including King Leopold III, who lived in a beautiful palace nearby.

"At least you can still work," Henri told his father. "I can't go to school anymore. I feel completely lost. I'll get up in the morning, and then what? Most of my friends are classmates who live in other parts of the city, and now I won't be able to see them. I feel like I've been left on a desert island."

The next day, Henri called his good friend Marcel Sobolski to complain. "What will we do all day?" Henri asked.

"I don't know," Marcel replied. "Most of the fun I had was at school. I'm going to miss our friends. I wish there was a way we could see each other."

"I've got an idea," said Henri, brightening up. "Let's get a bunch of our Jewish classmates together and we'll start a group. We'll call ourselves the Jewish Student Group, and we'll meet somewhere on a regular basis and talk and laugh."

A week later, two dozen boys and girls from various schools met for the first time. What started as a small, intimate gathering soon grew to nearly a hundred young Jews. It eventually became more than just a social group; it turned into a secret network of students risking their lives to help other members and strangers.

For nearly a year, they met in the clearing of a forest twice a week. Henri chose the site because it was remote and the group was unlikely to attract the Nazis' attention. The students came from different sections of the city, taking streetcars to the entrance of the Bois de la Cambre, the largest park in Brussels, and hiking through its woods to the clearing.

When they got together, they chatted and laughed and cried. Strangers at first, they quickly bonded and formed strong friendships in the darkest moments of their young lives. They sat on the ground and talked about themselves, most using only their first names. There were all kinds — outgoing students like Mirjam and serious ones like Bella; those like Leo whose souls burned with anger and those like Sara whose hearts ached from grief; immigrants from Germany and Poland whose families had fled the Nazis, like Sascha and Goldie; children of the well-to-do who had lost most everything, like Irma; and Henri's younger brother Jack and their fun-loving cousin Paula. All shared their hopes for the future — and their fears there wouldn't be one. Most important, they gave one another understanding and support. There was strength in numbers and comfort in sharing. For fun, they played childhood games and took countless pictures of one another, often in silly poses. The horsing around and joking made them forget, if only for a few hours, the emotional pain and hardships they were forced to endure as persecuted Jews.

Although they despised and feared the Nazis,

they were unaware of the looming horrors that would soon endanger the Jewish Student Group and all the Jews of Belgium.

For now, though, just being together felt good.

The group elected Marcel president, partly because he, along with Henri, had founded it and partly because Marcel was the son of a powerful man who had some influence with the Nazis. Marcel's father was a member of the *Judenrat*, a council of appointed Jews who carried out, in the Jewish community, the orders of the Nazis.

Henri was voted vice president. Although he was only five feet five, the dark-haired, brown-eyed youth maintained a large presence in the group. He made a point of talking to everyone, knowing just what to say to cheer someone up. Although he didn't date any of the girls, he still felt close to them.

Bella Blitz, fourteen, was chosen as secretary. Religious, quiet, serious, and smart, she had the respect of the others. Through her own efforts, she managed to introduce about seventy students to the group. She took her position as secretary seriously, writing notes even though no official business ever took place. Bella made sure that everyone had the phone numbers of the three leaders, and she gathered the numbers of the rest who had phones.

As the months passed, the tension among the young Jews increased.

"It's only a matter of time before the Nazis come and take us away," Bella told Henri. "I can feel it in my bones. I don't think my family and I will survive the war."

"Things will change for the better," Henri said, putting his arm around her. "You'll see." Then, standing up and raising his voice so the others could hear, he said, "Let's just enjoy one another's company."

"Hey, everyone," said Mirjam, whose ever ready smile always brightened the day, "let's play Telephone."

Amid groans and giggles, everyone lined up. Then Mirjam playfully whispered to the person next to her, "Henri and Rachel plan to run away to Switzerland and get married." That person then whispered the message to the next, and on down the line until it reached Sara, the last person, who announced, "The message is that Mirjam and Marcel are going steady and plan to sneak on a boat and escape to America."

Mirjam shrieked in embarrassment and then covered her mouth when she realized she was too loud. "I did *not* say that!"

Jack good-naturedly stuck an elbow into the ribs of Marcel, who was turning red. Everyone could tell Marcel and Mirjam liked each other, although the couple refused to publicly admit it.

Before the group left for the day, Bella, who seldom smiled although she had a big heart, asked for quiet. "I'd like to offer a prayer." Everyone stood and bowed their heads while she prayed for an end to the war.

In the spring of 1942, the Nazis ordered Belgium's 65,000 Jews to wear a yellow Star of David. Henri refused because, he told his parents, "If I did, I'd feel ashamed, like I was an outcast." Jack, who looked up to his older brother, also declined. But to ease their worried parents, who did wear the Star, the boys let their mother, Minka, sew a yellow star on each of their jackets — just in case. Their jackets were seldom worn.

Later that summer, during dinner, the family was talking about the summonses that had been sent to 10,000 Jewish people to report for "labor mobilization" at a work camp in the town of Malines, located between Brussels and Antwerp.

"I think it's great that most of the Jews refused to go," said Henri.

"Yes, but it's made the Nazis furious," his father,

Abram, replied. "The SS police have changed their tactics. Rather than telling the Jews to show up, they're forcing them."

Just then, the phone rang. Minka answered it, paused, and then let out a cry. "The Nazis grabbed Paula!" she wailed to her family. Seventeen-year-old Paula Lasman was Henri's favorite and closest cousin. Her mother was Minka's sister and partner in the family business.

"How did it happen?" asked Henri.

"Paula was on the train to Antwerp to spend a few days buying merchandise for us. But the Nazis stopped the train and took off all the Jews and transported them to the camp in Malines. They were given postcards and pencils so they could ask their families for money, food, and other supplies. That's how her family found out."

Every two or three weeks, Paula sent a postcard assuring everyone that she was doing well. She wrote that because she could speak and write in the three major languages of Belgium — French, German, and Flemish (a form of Dutch) — the Nazis had given her a job in the office.

After being shown Paula's latest postcard, Marcel told Henri, "I heard some disturbing news from the underground about Malines. The conditions are pretty bad there. It's surrounded with barbed wire and there's not enough food. Paula can't write about it because the Nazis are censoring all the mail. These letters are a trick. The Germans want the prisoners' families to think they're doing well at the camp. The letters are ways for the Nazis to get addresses of Jewish families. And the packages of food and money that families send? The prisoners seldom get any of them because the Germans take the packages themselves."

A few weeks later, Paula sent Henri a postcard dated September 14, 1942. It read:

Dear Family,

Keep healthy and strong. I think very often of you, my loved ones. It is my destiny. Hopefully, we will see each other shortly again. From your cousin who thinks of you.

Cousin Paula

Henri had a sickening feeling in the pit of his stomach. "She's trying to send us a clue," he told his parents. "The sentence 'It is my destiny' means that she knows something is going to happen to her. But what that is, I don't know — except I think it's bad news."

Reports soon filtered back to the Zylbermincs of

massive arrests of Jews in various neighborhoods in Antwerp and Brussels.

"It's only a matter of time before the Nazis come for us," Abram told his family. "We must go into hiding now."

Henri understood. His parents were petrified every minute of the day that the Nazis would arrest them. The fear they felt for their sons' safety as well as their own consumed them so much that it affected their very being. They hardly ate or laughed. They couldn't relax, and their bodies jerked at the slightest sound. *Yes, it's time to hide — for them,* he thought.

The Zylbermincs met with Father Bruno Reynders, a Benedictine monk who was playing a pivotal role in hiding hundreds of Jewish refugees, including many children, in orphanages, churches, and convents.

"I work closely with the underground organization Jewish Defense Council, and I've built a network of Belgians who are hiding Jews in the homes of Christian families in cities and on farms," Father Bruno told the Zylbermincs. "I also raise money from wealthy Belgians to provide the host families with food ration cards as well as other living expenses."

"Can you help us?" Abram asked.

"Yes. I can arrange for you and Minka to hide with a Catholic family. But there is room for only the two of you."

"What about our children?" asked Abram. "We can't leave them."

"I can place Paul in a monastery," said the monk. "He'll be safe there."

"Oh, thank you," said Minka. She hesitated at first and then asked, "Will he be taking Catholic religious instruction?"

"Mrs. Zylberminc, we are responsible for the lives of these children, but their souls don't belong to us," Father Bruno assured her. "Now, it's going to take a little longer to find a place for Jack and Henri."

"Father Bruno," Henri interrupted, "I don't want to be hidden. I can't wait out this war in a closet. I need to be active. I can do more good by helping my friends and others. I know how to take care of myself. After all, I'm eighteen."

"I want to stay with Henri," Jack piped up. "I don't want to be hidden, either."

With much reluctance, Abram and Minka agreed to let their two oldest sons fend for themselves, but with assistance from Father Bruno's network.

Turning to Henri, the monk said, "You need an extra pair of eyes, someone to help you out. I am going to assign this task to Tony. He's a good boy, a Catholic, an orphan, a smart kid. You'll like him. And I'll get you and Jack fake identity papers."

Once the arrangements were made for the two older boys to have their living expenses paid for, it was time for the family to split up. Not one to show much emotion, Abram told Henri and Jack, "This is just the way it has to be for now. But it shouldn't be for too long. And soon we'll be back together as a family again." They all hugged, but following Abram's lead, they shed no tears.

A young monk took Paul. Abram and Minka left with a member of Father Bruno's network. For everyone's protection, Henri and Jack were not told where their parents were being taken.

By now, Henri had heard that the Nazis were surrounding several major Jewish neighborhoods, breaking into homes and arresting every Jew they found, from infants to the sick and elderly, and trucking them to Malines.

Over the next few weeks, fewer and fewer members of the Jewish Student Group went to the forest clearing. Henri talked it over with Marcel, and they both reached the same conclusion.

At the next gathering, Henri announced, "We can't meet anymore — it's too dangerous. As you know, Marcel's father is a member of the *Judenrat*, and he's learned that the Nazis' current campaign of fear and terror is only going to get worse."

"What can we do?" asked Leo.

"Stay out of sight," Henri replied. "Don't get caught. Everyone has to find a way to hide or run away or do something to avoid being taken away. If not, hope for the best."

"Are you going to hide?" asked Annia.

"No, Jack and I will take our chances. We'll be careful and use our home as a base. It's empty and in a good location — the royal district — so the Germans aren't likely to raid the area anytime soon. You can use my place as a safe house. It's at 49 Rue Marie Christine in Laeken. If you're on the street and need a place to stay, go to the back of the house. The door is always unlocked. Also, if anybody needs something like food or clothes, write or call me or Marcel, and we'll try to get it."

Marcel made sure everyone there knew how to get in touch with him. "I carry a special permit because of my father's position on the *Judenrat*, so if I'm stopped by the Nazis, they'll let me go. I'm in the best position to try to get food and supplies to —"

He stopped talking when Sylvia, one of the members of the group, showed up in tears. "They got

Bella!" she sobbed. "The Nazis took Bella and her whole family!"

Every other day, it seemed, Henri learned of another friend who had been hauled away by the Nazis. Rachel. Leo. Sascha. Herbert. As the numbers mounted, so did the determination to help others. And to survive.

Operating out of their house, Henri and Jack would learn of their friends' needs from messengers, letters, and phone calls. Henri would give Tony money to buy food on the black market. Tony, usually accompanied by his brown-and-white mutt, Franci, would deliver the supplies twice a week. The tall blond Belgian never mentioned why he was willing to help; he just did. He never asked Henri about his life, and for that matter, Henri never asked Tony about his. Although they never had deep discussions, they grew to like each other.

On an early October afternoon, Henri returned home to find Mirjam in the living room, visibly shaken. "Mirjam, what's wrong?"

"The Gestapo raided my home last night," she blurted out. "When I heard them break open the door, I locked myself in the bathroom. They went through the whole apartment and took my sister, brother, and parents. I'm safe only because the

Gestapo forgot to check the bathroom. When they left, I ran over here. Henri, I'm never going to see my family again, am I?"

"Don't say that. You don't know for sure."

"It's so unfair, so cruel," she moaned. "We've been running from the Nazis for three years, ever since we fled from our home in Germany. We thought we'd be safe in Belgium. Henri, what am I going to do now?"

"You can stay here for as long as you like."

Mirjam remained at the house for two weeks until Marcel's father got her a teaching job with room and board at a Jewish orphanage in Brussels.

For the next couple of weeks, Henri stayed away from the house. He and Jack spent time with non-Jewish friends during the day and met with fellow Jews, like Marcel, who were coordinating ways to help others in need. It was risky to walk the streets at night, especially when the Nazis were driving around in black cars, called Opals, looking for curfew violators. But the Germans tended to take the same routes every night at the same time, so the brothers knew when and where it was best to walk. Sometimes, they felt safer sleeping under a bridge.

In late October, Henri and Jack returned to the house and collected the mail. "Jack, look at this!"

exclaimed Henri, holding up a makeshift envelope. "It's from Bella!" The envelope was nothing more than a piece of paper that had been tightly folded onto itself at the corners without any glue or tape. Inside was a photograph of Bella and a two-page letter written in French in pencil and dated Saturday, September 27, 1942. It read:

Dear Henri,

I am writing this letter to you from the train. . . . As I predicted, my parents, my brother, and I were caught in the raid. On Thursday night, the Gestapo came to our house; they opened and broke through the front door of the house next to ours and they entered our house through the roof. This done, they gave us ten minutes to pack our bags.

Once we got to Malines, we noticed that we were missing many things. On the other hand, for bread, we had only a half loaf for four people; we had forgotten the rest on the table at home, which shows you how upset we were. What atrocities at Malines! Children, from four months old to all ages, were crying. They are given only a little milk each day. The adults are starving to death. A quarter of a loaf of bread for the whole day and a little black coffee at morning and at night. At noon they give us some soup, but what a soup! Since I hadn't eaten anything all day long I had a few spoonfuls. But I had such a stomachache from it that I suffered all night long and the next day also. They searched us and took everything: money, passports, pocketknives. At that time, there were only 180 people in the barracks. Then, every half hour, cars came with people from Liège, Brussels . . . then at night a large group came from Antwerp. We thought that we were going to stay until noon, so we asked to be able to write to people to bring us some bread, but unfortunately we left the next day at four in the morning. On Thursday, there were 180 people in the convoy; on Saturday, 3,000. Rachel is here with us.

We don't know where we are going.

In any case, we have been traveling for four days, and for this journey received only one loaf of bread — just enough not to starve. The little children cry all day long. People caught Friday in the street don't even have a spare shirt — nothing at all. They were going to receive packages, but we left too soon. I heard that they were going to deport all Jews from Belgium. So, be careful and hide well so that they don't catch you. I'm sending you my most recent photo; I hope you'll print it and distribute it to the people I know. I'm throwing this letter out the window in the hopes that it will reach its destination. Think sometimes of your friend Bella. Greetings to everybody.

Bella

With a trembling hand, Henri gazed at the photo. It was a school picture of Bella, posing with a faint smile, her thick dark hair cascading down her back. He turned the photo over. Bella had written, "I am dedicating this photograph to my friend Henri in very sad times. But I hope there will be a second photo in better times. Think sometimes of Bella who wishes you courage and hope. See you soon, Bella."

Henri began shedding tears for the horrors that Bella and the others were going through. When he regained his composure, he told Jack, "Do you know what this means? Malines is not a work camp; it's a holding camp. The Jews who are being rounded up aren't working there. It's just a place to process Jews before they're deported from Belgium. They're being taken somewhere else — probably out of the country. That's what Paula was trying to tell us, but she couldn't."

"We haven't heard anything from Paula since her postcard in August," said Jack.

"I know. This is bad, very bad."

"I wish I knew Bella better."

"Me, too, Jack. She's always so serious, but she has a good heart. Look at what she did. She ignored her own terrible situation to sound the alarm to her friends."

Jack studied the handmade envelope and said, "There's no stamp." He pointed to where Bella had written in French: *"port payé par le destinataire"* (postage paid by receiver). "If she threw it out the window of a moving train and it had no stamp, how did it ever end up here?" Jack asked.

"It's a miracle!" Henri declared. "Somebody must have found it on the tracks and dropped it in a mailbox. It's unbelievable that this envelope was able to make it all the way to the main post office in Brussels. All foreign or suspicious mail is supposed to be turned over to the Nazi administration. But that couldn't have happened. I bet that some postal employee who handled the letter realized the importance of it and must have delivered it himself. Jack, it's fate. This letter was supposed to get here."

Henri broke down again. "I feel like crying all day," he blubbered, "but that won't do me any good. Besides, Bella wrote to me because she knew that as a leader of the group, I would get in touch with the others. We need to tell as many friends as possible about the conditions at Malines, the trains, and the deportations. We must warn them that under no circumstances should they believe the Nazis are sending them to labor camps. The Jews must hide."

For the next several nights, Henri and Jack

sneaked over to the homes of all the friends who didn't have phones and warned them. The brothers told Tony, who went into sections of Brussels that were the most dangerous for Jews and informed people about the deportations. Marcel called those friends who had phones.

Henri couldn't stop thinking about Bella's letter: *In the most horrible days of her life, she still thinks of others. I must save this letter for posterity.* In the attic of his house, he built a little hiding place and stored important letters, family documents, and cherished photographs that were given to him by members of the group.

Although Nazi raids on Jewish homes were increasing, Henri and Jack passed up chances to go into hiding because they wanted to keep the family residence as a safe house and communications center. But they took precautions in case they needed to make a quick escape. They always slept in their clothes and shoes. Henri slept only three or four hours a night and yet remained so aware during his light sleep that the smallest noise would wake him up.

"Jack, we must be alert with every step we take," Henri reminded him. "One mistake and we'll be deported to God knows where. No matter where you are or what you're doing, make sure that you always have an escape route."

Late one night while Marcel was sleeping over with the brothers, which he did occasionally, the three were chatting in an upstairs room with the lights out. Marcel was telling them how well Mirjam had been doing at the orphanage. "She's terrific with the children," Marcel said. "They love her."

"We know someone else who's pretty sweet on her, too," said Henri.

"Yeah," added Jack. "We hear through the grapevine that you visit the orphanage an awful lot."

"And it's not just to find out how the kids are doing," added Henri.

"Hey, quit kidding around," said Marcel. "I won't be seeing her anymore — at least not until the war is over."

"Why not?" asked Henri.

"There's a rumor going around — one that my father thinks is true — that the Nazis are getting ready to deport all the Jews from old age homes and orphanages. So Mirjam volunteered to escort twelve kids from the orphanage all the way to Switzerland. She'll use the help of the Belgium and French underground."

"She's very courageous," said Henri.

Marcel nodded. "Mirjam left with the children a few days ago. I pray she makes it there safely."

Just then, they heard the screeching of car tires outside. Henri peered out the window. Two black Opals had pulled up in front of the house. "Gestapo!" he whispered. "To the roof!"

The three young men darted up to the attic and dived out a window onto the roof. Seconds later, the Gestapo sprang through an attic door and onto the connecting roof of the next-door neighbor's house. "Halt or we'll shoot!" one of the officers yelled.

"Keep running!" shouted Henri to Jack and Marcel, who were scrambling behind him. He hadn't even finished saying the words before gunfire erupted. As bullets flew past him, Henri reached the edge of the roof. He dangled over the side, grabbed the drainpipe, and slid down to a small courtyard below. He waited while the others followed his lead. Then they sneaked into the basement of another house and hid.

"I-I th-thought we were g-going to d-die," stammered Jack, unable to stop his trembling. "I didn't th-think th-there was a way out on th-that roof."

"You forget that I always have an escape plan," said Henri.

"Do you think the Gestapo knows what we've been doing?" asked Marcel.

Henri shrugged. "Maybe one of us was followed. We'll have to be more careful. This was a very close call."

They spent the night in the basement, catching only a couple hours of sleep. In the morning, Henri rubbed his eyes and stared at his brother.

"Jack, your hair!" Henri exclaimed.

"Yeah, what about it?"

"It's turned white!"

The terror from being shot at had transformed Jack's dark brown hair into a dusty pale gray.

Despite the narrow escape, Henri often went back to the house, but only late at night to pick up the mail and see if there were friends who needed help. Some members of the Jewish Student Group used the house as a place to hide temporarily until they could get fake documents. Once they had the papers, they planned to flee to Switzerland, which was a neutral country. Unfortunately, the list of names of the group's members who had been captured by the Nazis kept getting longer.

Henri wasn't worried about not wearing a yellow star, because Father Bruno had given him a set of fake identity papers. They included a birth certificate that said he was Pierre Faucher; a certificate that said he was baptized a Catholic; and a work permit that said he was an employee of a Belgian company that made fur coats for the German officers. Although Henri was always on the alert for the police and Gestapo when he was walking, there were several times when he couldn't avoid them, and he was stopped and questioned. But after showing the authorities his papers, he was always allowed to go on his way — except once.

"I don't know if this work permit is valid anymore," said one of three Belgian Nazis who were examining Henri's documents after he had been rounded up in a raid on the street. "We must check this out. Come with us, Pierre."

Henri was worried, for good reason. The Nazis were combing the streets looking for young people to ship to forced labor camps for the German war effort. *If they discover my permit is a fake, they'll deport me,* he thought.

The police took him to their headquarters on the second floor of an office building. On a piece of paper, one of the officers jotted down the number of Henri's work permit. "I'm going to call the office of the German administrator of labor and see if this number is still valid," the officer told "Pierre." "For your sake, I hope it is." Then he left, locking the door behind him.

I've got to get out of here before they find out it's phony, Henri told himself. He ran to the window and yanked on it. *Oh, thank God, it opens.* He looked down. It was at least twenty feet to the ground. *Don't worry how high you are. Jump!* He leaped out the window and landed hard on the concrete, causing him to tumble and wince in pain. He picked himself up and, half running and half limping, hurried down the street and hopped onto a passing streetcar.

When he returned home, Henri found Marcel sitting in a chair, his eyes red and blank. "Marcel, are you okay?"

"No," he muttered. "Mirjam didn't make it."

"What happened?"

"We got a report from the underground that Mirjam and the children sneaked out of Belgium and through France. They made it all the way to the Swiss border, but then they got arrested. We don't know exactly how. They were either turned over to the Germans by a French collaborator, or the Swiss border guards wouldn't let the children in and the Germans caught them. We don't know where they've been taken."

After Marcel left the house, Henri went up into

the attic. There was something he wanted to do. He opened the lid to the little hiding place where he kept his important documents and letters. He pulled out a photograph of Mirjam and stared at it. *You didn't have to volunteer, Mirjam,* he thought. *You didn't have to risk your life. You could've stayed hidden here or in a convent or somewhere safer. God, I hope you and the children survive.*

He flipped the photograph over to read what she had written on the back: "Souvenir for my best friend whom I always love. From a friend who hopes you will think of her often. For Henri, my dear friend, from Mirjam. 10 October 1942. Brussels."

He reached into the hiding place and selected dozens of other photos of Jewish Student Group members. Some of the pictures were of Jack and him, their arms around several girls. Others were professional pictures taken at a studio and given to him as mementos.

In the dim light of the attic, Henri selected photos of friends from the group who had been nabbed by the Nazis. He gazed longingly at each picture and read what that person had inscribed to him on the back. Raven-haired, wide-eyed Annia: "The most beautiful rose will one day lose its beauty. True friendship stays forever." Sixteen-year-old Irma, who looked and acted much older than her age: "I hope this picture will give you as much pleasure as I can offer to you from my heart. From a very good friend who will never forget you." Leo, clad in a sport coat, tie, and slacks: "For Henri, as a souvenir of good comradeship and good friendship." Studious, bespectacled Herbert in a formal pose: "Steel and iron cannot destroy our friendship. In remembrance of the friendly hours spent in sad times in the year 1942." One after the other, Henri studied the pictures. He choked up when he cast his eyes on a photo of Paula smiling brightly as she walked down the street flanked by Henri and Jack. Tears trickled off his chin after he looked at several group shots that included Bella. *Are all of you holding up okay?* he wondered. *Are you able to cope with the suffering? Will I ever see any of you again? Are you even alive?*

In the spring of 1944, the Allied forces were bombing the rail lines and factories of Belgium. Air raid sirens blared constantly in Brussels, warning everyone to seek safety in bomb shelters. During one such raid, Henri hustled into a shelter with forty other people, including several German officers, shortly before a bomb struck the building. Later, when the people tried to leave, they discovered that debris had blocked the only exit. Henri and the others spent hours removing the rubble, chunk by chunk, until finally they were able to squeeze their way out. It was long past curfew as Henri scurried from one shadow to the next on his way back home.

"Jack," he told his brother when he arrived, "it's time for us to go into hiding. Everyone we've been helping has either been taken away or has gone underground. With all the bombing going on now, it's just too dangerous to be on the streets."

"Where will we go?" asked Jack.

"We'll live with Mama and Papa."

"But we don't know where they're hiding."

"I'll find out."

The next day, he met with Tony. "I need to know where my parents are hiding," Henri told him.

"You know I can't tell you that, for their safety and yours."

"Jack and I must be with them. It's our only hope of surviving. The Gestapo is starting to raid this neighborhood. Nazis are everywhere, and if they don't get us, the bombs will. Tony, please."

Tony nodded. "I understand." After a moment of thought, he said, "Your parents are safe in the home of a Christian family in the French section. I'll take you and Jack there. But the people in the house must not know about you two or they might get too nervous and demand that your parents leave."

"Thank you, Tony. You're a lifesaver. We couldn't have survived this long without you."

That evening, Tony led Henri and Jack to the house. They slipped into the back door and tiptoed up the staircase to the attic, where an armoire stood against a far wall. Tony walked over to it and opened the door. It was empty. But when he pushed on a panel, the back of the armoire swung up. Tony motioned for them to step through.

They did, and entered a tiny, windowless room where, in the light from a lantern, they saw the shock on their parents' faces. Abram and Minka gasped in astonishment and then quietly wept and hugged their sons. After hearing Henri explain why he and Jack had come, Abram said, "No matter what happens now, we might as well all be here together and hope for the best. God willing, we'll make it."

The host family, who lived below them, never knew Jack and Henri were hiding with Abram and Minka. The boys remained in the cramped hideout — which had a toilet and sink but no stove — until the Germans were driven out of the city six months later. They survived on sandwiches and canned goods delivered regularly by Tony.

On September 3, 1944, the Zylbermincs heard cheering in the streets and church bells ringing. "It can only mean one thing," said Henri. "Brussels has been liberated!"

He and Jack raced downstairs and ran outside, where people were dancing in the street and waving to American and British soldiers who were roaring triumphantly into the city. Henri told his parents, "You go home. Jack and I will show up later." Like hundreds of thousands of Belgians, the brothers celebrated for several days in a delirious sea of people hugging and kissing and cheering. Henri lost Jack after the first day and didn't see him again until they each staggered home, exhausted but jubilant.

"I can't describe how happy I feel to be free and no longer afraid," Henri told his family. "The only thing that could make me happier is if all the members of the group could one day soon get back together again."

It would be another eight months before the war in Europe officially ended. During that time, the world began seeing the horrors of concentration camps and slave labor camps. Henri's hope of a reunion of the Jewish Student Group faded as he learned of the fate of its members.

The day after his cousin Paula had sent her final postcard to him, the one in which she wrote, "It is my destiny," she was put on a train with a thousand other Jews and shipped to the notorious concentration camp in Auschwitz, Poland, where she and the rest were killed.

Bella perished at Auschwitz, too, just days after she threw her letter to Henri out the train window, warning him of the deportations.

Mirjam and the children she guided never returned. Neither did Leo and Sascha and Rachel and Herbert and Annia and Irma. Out of the nearly 100 members of the group, Henri found only eleven who survived the war.

Every time Henri learned of the death of another member, it felt like an invisible knife twisting deeper into his heart. To ease the pain, he had to keep reminding himself, *We did what we could to help one another.* That's what the Jewish Student Group was all about.

After Brussels was liberated, Henri's youngest brother, Paul, who had been safely hidden in a Catholic monastery, was reunited with the family.

When the war ended, Henri attended the Academy of De-

sign in Brussels. In 1948, he married Bella Wunderman, who had been hidden in a convent during the war by Father Bruno's network.

In 1950, the entire Zylberminc family immigrated to the United States. Henri and Bella settled in California, where Henri changed his name to Harry Silvers and became an American citizen. He made a living as a businessman before becoming a custom furniture designer for film and television productions. Harry, who retired in 1992 and is a widower, has two sons and four grandchildren.

Today Harry volunteers at the Simon Wiesenthal Center's Museum of Tolerance, in Los Angeles. He has donated to the center his collection of photos and letters from the Jewish Student Group, including those written by Bella and Paula. They can be viewed on the Internet by going to **www.wiesenthal.com/library/dap.htm** and typing "teenagers" in the search engine.

Jack retired from the retail upholstery business that he owned and lives in California. Paul, who was an eye doctor for the United States Army, is a retired colonel living in Colorado.

Marcel Sobolski remained in Belgium after the war and took over the family jewelry business.

Despite his best efforts, Harry was unable to find out what happened to his "lifesaver," Tony.

For the hundreds of Jews he helped save, Father Bruno

Reynders was honored by Yad Vashem as one of the Righteous Among the Nations.

At the time of the German invasion, there were about 65,000 Jews in Belgium. An estimated 10,000 Jews fled to neighboring countries. Thanks to an amazingly active Belgian resistance movement, 25,000 Jews of all ages were hidden in private homes, convents, monasteries, churches, farms, and hospitals. Tragically, nearly 30,000 Jews — including most members of the Jewish Student Group — were deported to Auschwitz and murdered.

"There Must Be a Way to Save the Children"

HILDE JACOBSTHAL, HOLLAND, 1942–1943

When Hilde Jacobsthal entered the once majestic Hollandse Schouwburg (the Dutch Theater), she gasped at the appalling sight inside.

For more than fifty years, the three-story building, its front decorated with columns and arches, had stood proudly in the center of Amsterdam, Holland. It was here that some of Europe's finest entertainers had performed in front of formally dressed audiences who sat in plush velvet seats. But that was before the Nazis had invaded the country.

Now, two years later, in 1942, it was a theater showing a real-life drama of heartache, a wretched place where Jews who had been uprooted from their homes were forced to gather before the Nazis shipped them away.

When Hilde stepped inside, she couldn't believe her eyes. Gone were the rows of comfortable seats, the heavy curtains, and the dazzling light fixtures.

The Nazis had ripped out the seating so they could cram in as many Jews as possible. Hundreds of tired, scared families sat on the floor. Glum-faced men and women leaned on their suitcases while, at their side, small children whined or cried. The air was thick, sticky, and rank.

How awful, Hilde thought. *This looks and smells like a barn full of animals going to slaughter. Only these aren't animals. These are my people. What have the Nazis done to them?*

All the Jews in the theater were being sent to Westerbork, a Dutch camp. From there, no one knew where they would end up. The Nazis said that after Westerbork, the Jews would be shipped off to various work camps in Germany. The Nazis lied.

Hilde was a seventeen-year-old student nurse at the Crèche, a child-care center across the street from the theater, and there were limits to what she could do to help the soon-to-be deported children. But she did her best. She tried to comfort weeping youngsters by stroking their hair, singing a song, offering them an apple. Sometimes she received a smile in return, occasionally even a hug.

Hilde went back the next day, and the day after. As groups of Jews were moved out and new ones were moved in, Hilde felt overwhelmed and broken-hearted, as did other Crèche student nurses who also were trying to help.

There must be more that we can do, she thought. *There must be a way to save the children.* There was. Hilde just didn't know it yet.

Hilde was a German Jew born in Berlin in 1925. When she was three years old, Hilde, her father, Walter, her mother, Betty, and her seven-year-old brother, Jo, moved to Amsterdam. Walter thought the move would be good for his ready-to-wear clothing business. He was right — for a while.

Hilde enjoyed a happy childhood in Amsterdam, living in a comfortable home with her adoring family. By the time she reached her midteens, she had grown into a statuesque, curly-haired beauty. She was strong and athletic and, like many Dutch children, an expert swimmer. She dreamed of going to medical school and becoming a pediatrician because she loved children so much. In the meantime, she volunteered at a nearby day-care center just so she could be around toddlers and infants.

But her ambition took a fatal blow when the Nazis invaded Holland on May 10, 1940. Five days later, the Dutch surrendered. As her family watched

German troops march into Amsterdam, Hilde broke into tears and thought, *The Jews are about to face disaster.* Her mother fainted.

Under the iron-fisted control of the Nazis, conditions gradually worsened for the Dutch. Young men were sent to work camps. Everybody, including non-Jews, was made to carry identification cards, but Jews' IDs had a large *J* stamped on them. Jews could not work in civil service jobs, could not teach in the schools, or even play in orchestras. Jews could go only to Jewish hospitals and businesses. They could shop only in Jewish stores during restricted hours. Jewish children were kicked out of public schools. Jews were banned from trolleys, buses, movies, and restaurants. The Nazis took away their cars and bicycles.

Nothing owned by a Jew was safe, not even Hilde's old beat-up canoe. She had asked for one shortly after the Nazi invasion. "Hilde, the Nazis will never let a Jewish girl keep a canoe," Walter told her.

"But I want it so badly," she said. "I'll work hard and get the money myself. A used one won't cost so much."

Walter said nothing further. He didn't have the heart to argue with his sweet daughter. Hilde earned money by writing children's stories and selling them to a local newspaper. By the end of summer, she had earned enough guilders to buy an old canoe. Her father and brother painted it bright white.

The first day out on the Amstel River was like heaven for Hilde. Slicing through the water with strong, confident strokes, she forgot about the Nazis. Her joy didn't last long. A few weeks after she bought the canoe, her father received a phone call from the owner of the marina where Hilde kept her boat. "Walter, don't let your daughter come here anymore," said the owner. "It's too dangerous. The Nazis have taken the girl's canoe."

When Jewish children were banned from receiving a public education, they were allowed to attend special schools just for Jews, but Hilde wasn't interested. She wanted to enroll in the student nurse training program at the Crèche, a respected child-care center run by Jews. Hilde was only sixteen, two years younger than the required minimum age. But she managed to get an admissions interview anyway with the headmistress, Mrs. Henrietta Pimentel.

Impressed by Hilde's compassion for children as well as her good grades in high school and her volunteer work, Mrs. Pimentel bent the rules so

Hilde could join nineteen other student nurses in the two-year training course. Many university professors who had been fired because they were Jewish were now teaching at the center. Hilde knew that she would never get training like this anywhere else.

When she put on her uniform — a dark dress with white cuffs and white collar under a white apron and topped off by a white triangular-shaped nurse's cap — Hilde felt empowered. She believed that her love and concern for children would help get them through anything, from grief over a broken toy to the pain of a scraped elbow.

From eight in the morning to six in the evening, Hilde worked and learned at the Crèche. The children were fun. The instructors were excellent. And the other student nurses were kindred souls who shared her love of children. Music was Hilde's favorite subject. As part of their training, the nurses were taught to sing songs from all over the world. Hilde learned every folk song and children's tune she could and delighted her preschoolers with her warm, melodious voice that always managed to lift their spirits.

Hilde lived at the Crèche full-time during her training and went home on weekends. Because Jews were banned from public transportation and from owning bicycles, the walk home took hours. Sometimes in the cold weather Hilde would skate across the frozen canals, her uniform flowing out behind her in the wind. But then the Nazis banned Jews from ice-skating.

Life for Jewish people in Holland grew worse as more and more rights were taken from them. In April 1942, all Jews six years old and above were ordered to wear the yellow Star of David with the word "*Jood*" (Dutch for Jew) on their clothing. If non-Jews were caught talking with, entertaining, or even being polite to a Jew, they were threatened with severe punishment, including death.

"Hilde, there's no way I'm going to wear a yellow star," her brother, Jo, said. "It's not for me." That night he packed his bag and disappeared without even saying good-bye. No one knew where he went.

Despite the Nazis' cruel restrictions, Hilde and her friends tried to find ways to enjoy life. They would visit the ice cream shop or walk in the park. The teenage girls talked about important subjects like boys and fashion and movie stars, but soon the conversation would drift to less pleasant things, like Nazis ordering teenage Jews to report to work camps and families going into hiding.

One of Hilde's good friends was Margot Frank, the older daughter of a prominent Jewish business- man who knew Walter well. Margot's younger sis- ter, Anne, sometimes tagged along. Anne was a chatterbox and a bit annoying because she never stopped talking and always was asking questions about everybody and everything. Nevertheless, Hilde enjoyed being with Margot, including when they went to the synagogue on Sundays for a dis- cussion group.

But then one summer Sunday, Margot didn't show up; nor the following Sunday. Hilde went to the Franks' home. No one was there. Neighbors said the family had left; they didn't know where.

Hilde assumed they had gone into hiding. She wondered why her own family didn't hide or try to escape to a neutral country like Switzerland. For years, Walter had opened their home to refugees from Germany and Austria. During their stay at the Jacobsthals' before heading for South America or the United States, the guests gave accounts of Nazi ruthlessness. But Walter never tried to move his own family. He believed he had a responsibility to stay and help others. "Besides," he once told Hilde, "this lunacy can't last much longer. Holland will be freed soon. The British will arrive and push the Nazis out of here." By the time he realized he was wrong, it was too late to escape.

In July 1942, the deportation of Holland's Jews was underway. The Nazis gutted the Hollandse Schouwburg and turned the theater into a holding pen. Every day hundreds of Jews carrying a few bags with their belongings arrived there, replacing the Jews from the previous day who had been shipped off to Westerbork.

During their few, brief breaks at the Crèche, the student nurses would gaze out the window across the street and watch the Nazis herd frightened Jewish families into the theater.

"It must be awful in there," said Hilde's fellow student and good friend Sieny Kattenburg.

"Look at those sad, scared faces," said Hilde. "It breaks my heart."

"I feel so helpless. Isn't there anything we can do for them?"

"Let's go ask Mrs. Pimentel if it's possible to get into the theater to see how the children are holding up," Hilde suggested. "Maybe we can cheer them up by singing to them and bringing them something to eat."

A few days after hearing their request, Mrs. Pimentel received word from the Nazis that the student nurses could go inside the theater to comfort the children.

As Hilde walked toward the Hollandse Schouwburg, she thought back to happier days, when she dressed up and spent glorious evenings there with her parents, listening to lively music and laughing at comedians. She remembered the last shows she saw, which starred Jewish entertainers who had fled from Berlin and Vienna before the invasion. Because of his stature as a successful, well-known businessman, Hilde's father received special treatment, so after a show he would take the family backstage to meet the actors and singers. At times like that, Hilde fantasized about what it would be like to sing in the Hollandse Schouwburg.

Never had she imagined that it would be under such awful conditions as this. Now armed soldiers stood in front of the arched windows where, a few years earlier, theatergoers in their finery gathered before the show.

Halfway across the street, Hilde and the other nurses stopped when they heard the soldiers yelling and cursing at the Jews who were being hustled inside the theater. A wave of fear spread over Hilde as doctors, lawyers, teachers — the cream of Amsterdam's Jewish population — were spat on and called "filthy swine."

"What are the soldiers going to do to us when we walk past them?" Hilde asked Sieny.

"I don't know, but suddenly I'm very scared," Sieny replied.

"Me, too. Let's walk real fast and not make eye contact with them." Hilde took a deep breath and marched toward the entrance. As the student nurses reached the front steps, the soldiers stopped jeering. Unexpectedly, they said nothing at all to the young women. Seconds after the nurses passed them, the soldiers began hurling insults again to other Jews.

Sieny whispered to Hilde, "That's so odd. The soldiers know we're Jewish."

"Maybe our uniforms carry some respect," said Hilde. "I wish the Nazis would treat everyone else like they did us."

When she stepped inside, she was appalled at seeing so many people crammed into the smelly, stripped-down theater. Once she got over her initial shock, Hilde walked up to the first family she saw and handed an apple to a boy who was crying and hiding his face in his mother's blouse. Hilde stepped over to another child, a whimpering toddler, and started softly humming a lullaby. She continued to sing to many other kids. She did this every day for the next two weeks.

Hilde believed her efforts helped soothe the young-sters, but she had no illusion that this was good enough. "There must be more that we can do," she told Viri Cohen, the nurse in charge of the interns.

Days later, Viri led the student nurses to the the-ater and said to the Nazi officer in charge, "We're going to pick a few children and take them back with us across the street and give them real meals and a place to sleep overnight."

"Why should we allow you to do that?" the officer asked.

"Because maybe they won't cry so much. It'll be better for everyone. We'll bring the children back in the morning when you need them."

The officer glanced over at the student nurses, who flashed him lovely smiles. He nodded. "All right," he said.

Once inside, Viri told Hilde, "We can pick forty children; that's all we can handle. You must ask the parents if it's all right with them for us to take the children for the night. If so, bring the children over to the Crèche."

Hilde looked around and spotted a small dark-haired boy who was clinging to his mother. His eyes were wide from worry, but he wasn't crying. After Hilde introduced herself to the mother and explained why she was there, she asked, "What is your boy's name?"

"Willie," the woman replied.

"Hello, Willie," Hilde said to the boy. "How old are you?"

Willie pushed his head into his mother's skirt and peeked up at Hilde with a shy smile.

"He's four," his mother replied. Turning to her son, she said, "Willie, this nice girl is going to take you across the street for something good to eat and to spend the night with other children. It's okay. Go with her. She'll bring you back in the morning."

Hilde held out her hand. Willie grabbed it and squeezed tightly. Then Hilde went to another family and, like the other student nurses, continued to gather children. Soon they had a cluster of boys and girls, some sniffling and uneasy about leaving their parents behind. To calm them, Hilde sang during their walk across the street.

At the Crèche, the children were given hot meals. The playroom had been transformed into a huge dormitory where forty army cots were laid end to end. Although the room was crowded, it was better than being packed on the floor all night in the stuffy theater.

"Miss Hilde," asked Willie, "what's going to happen to me and Mama?"

Hilde knelt on the floor to be at eye level with him. "Tomorrow, you're going on a train ride out into the country, to a place where your mommy can get a job." *How else can I answer him?* she told herself. *Tell him that he's going to a work camp where conditions no doubt are a lot worse than they are here? Tell him that the Nazis are likely to treat his mother and him badly?*

"But I want to go home," he whined.

"I know you do, Willie. Maybe you'll get to go home soon." Then, standing up to face the group of children, she said, "Hey, everyone, let's do something fun!"

To keep the children's minds off their desperate situation, Hilde taught them a song from the opera *Hansel and Gretel* and then had them act out the words:

"Brother, come and dance with me,
Both my hands I offer thee,
Right foot first,
Left foot then,
'Round about and back again."

At bedtime, Hilde sang lullabies in German, English, and Dutch until the little ones had fallen asleep. The next day, she escorted the children back to the theater and returned them to their parents. As she walked away, she looked back at Willie. He smiled and waved at her. She thought her heart would break.

Several days later, Viri Cohen summoned Hilde and three other interns, including Hilde's friend Sieny. Viri brushed away a few strands of graying hair from her glasses. For a woman with a gentle, sweet manner, she seemed unusually tense. "You're our most reliable girls, so I'm going to ask you to do something that must remain a secret," she said. "It's part of a plan to save some of these children. But I must warn you, it's dangerous. If you're caught, it could cost you your life — and in fact, everyone else's at the Crèche."

"If it means a chance to actually save children, count me in," declared Hilde. The others murmured in agreement.

"What is it we have to do?" Sieny asked.

"We're going to get some of these children out of here and secretly place them with families so they can avoid being deported," Viri replied.

"Where?" Hilde asked.

"In Christian homes, where the children will be given Christian names and raised as Christians. Maybe that way the Nazis will leave them alone."

"Which children will be picked?" asked Hilde.

"Leave that to me for now. Just know that we won't take away any child whose parents haven't agreed to give up their child to another family for the duration of the war. Tonight I'll pick one of the children. Hilde, at midnight, someone will come to the back door. Your job will be to get the child, make his bed so it looks like he's still asleep in it, keep him quiet, and then hand him over to the person."

"Won't the Nazis find out in the morning that a child is missing?" Hilde asked.

"No, because we're purposely keeping incomplete lists of the names of the children who are staying here."

"Will we be taking babies out of here?" asked Sieny.

"Not right now, because they might cry and alert the Nazis. For the immediate future, it will be toddlers. You must be very careful and do it quickly. The child can't make a sound, so it might be best to cover his face with a blanket." Viri paused a moment. "One more thing. You must not say anything to anyone. I know we can depend on you."

The job didn't sound very hard, but deep down Hilde knew how great the danger was. The old theater was crawling with Nazis. If a child cried while being transferred, the Nazis could find out. It wasn't unusual for the Gestapo to go into the Crèche at night to make sure there was a child in every cot.

Hilde was afraid, but at the same time it was something she wanted to do, something she *had* to do. So just before midnight, she stepped quietly into the playroom and picked up a four-year-old girl who had been pointed out by Viri. Hilde used rolled-up blankets and two teddy bears to make it look like a child was asleep in the bed.

Carrying the sleepy girl who was bundled so that her face was covered, Hilde walked quietly down the stairs that led out to the back garden. There, she spotted a figure in the shadows. Hilde couldn't tell if it was a man or a woman. The figure stepped forward, grabbed the child, and slipped away into the night. Not a word was spoken during the exchange.

The next morning, a German soldier arrived at the Crèche and told Hilde, "We need the children. Their parents are leaving today. Bring them over now."

As she led the children to the theater, she wondered, *What will I do if he notices that there are thirty-*

nine children instead of forty? she asked herself. *Will he go berserk and take it out on me or the children? Will he order the Crèche destroyed? I can't think like that. Just act natural.* To her relief, the soldier didn't bother to count.

In addition to providing some comfort to the children in the gloomy, overcrowded theater every day, Hilde and three other student nurses each had a special job to do, a difficult one. She had to convince Jewish parents to turn their children over to complete strangers, Christians no less, until hopefully they could all be reunited when the Nazis were driven out of Holland.

When the Crèche received word that a Christian family was willing to act as a secret foster family, Hilde would seek out parents of a young child or two. It was no easy task to ask permission of the parents to release their child into the care of strangers. Hilde had to be careful that a Nazi collaborator wasn't eavesdropping or that the parents, upset over the thought of giving up their child, would create a scene. There was no easy way for her to know how parents would react to such a radical, desperate plan, but Hilde had to try.

"Your daughter, Tina, is doing fine at the Crèche," Hilde told the mother of a three-year-old. "We'll bring her back tomorrow when you're shipped out to Westerbork or" — she lowered her voice before speaking again — "we can see to it that she isn't deported."

"What do you mean?" asked the mother.

"We can arrange to have Tina hidden in a good home." Hilde then explained the scheme.

"You want me to leave Tina behind?" the mother said in disbelief. "No, I could never be separated from my child. I couldn't take the chance of never finding my baby again. No, no, no. That's a terrible plan. The Nazis are sending us away to a work camp. It's not like they're going to kill us. No, we'll face whatever we must together."

"I understand," Hilde said softly. "I'll bring Tina to you in the morning."

As she returned to the Crèche, Hilde wondered what she would do if she were in the same position as Tina's mother. *I don't think I'd have the strength and faith to willingly give up my young child to perfect strangers. Before I'd hand her over, I'd have to be very desperate and convinced that keeping her meant her death. And even then, it would be an unbearable decision.*

But for every turndown, there were other parents — especially German refugees who already had witnessed Nazi brutality — willing to let go of their children. Like Asher and Maya Braun, parents of Eddie, who was three, and Rita, who was only eighteen months old.

When Hilde received word that a Christian couple had agreed to take in two young siblings, she went to the theater to search for the right family. She found the Brauns and whispered to them that their children could be safely hidden.

Tears welled up in Maya's eyes as she looked at her husband. He swallowed hard and said, "Who knows what horrors await us at the hands of the Nazis? They're monsters. Why put our children through all this and risk their lives? The Nazis could just as easily take them away from us at the work camp. At least, if we give them up now, our children have a chance at survival."

Maya put her hands on her face, struggling to keep her composure. "Okay, Asher, but let's not tell the children. It's better if they don't know, at least not here." Turning to Hilde, she said, "Tell them later."

"I will," said Hilde.

Maya and Asher took the children in their arms and held them, knowing that it could be for the last time.

"Mama, are you crying?" asked Eddie.

Maya wiped away her tears. "Oh, I'm just a little sad because we have to stay in this awful place tonight. But guess what?" she said, in a fake cheery voice. "You and Rita get to go with Miss Hilde to a very nice place across the street."

"Yes," said Hilde. "You'll be with other children, and you'll get to eat some good food, and then we'll play games and sing songs. Would you like that?"

Eddie nodded. So did Rita, who liked to mimic her big brother.

As Hilde took the children's hands, Asher put on a brave smile. "Now you two go have fun."

Maya blurted, "Mama and Papa love you. We love you. We love you."

Guiding the children out of the theater, Hilde glanced back at the Brauns. Maya and Asher had their heads buried in each other's chests, sobbing.

At the Crèche, just before bedtime, Hilde told the children that they were going on a little trip. "You'll be staying with a nice Dutch family who are very much looking forward to taking care of you," Hilde said.

"Are Mama and Papa going to be there, too?" Eddie asked.

"No, honey, they aren't. They have to go away for

a while. But then they'll be back and everything will be fine again."

Eddie started to cry. Seeing her brother in tears, Rita began bawling, too. Hilde kept assuring them that everything would turn out fine. She and Sieny then rocked them and began softly singing, "Hush, Little Baby, Don't You Cry" until the children fell sound asleep. A few hours later, the children were in the arms of rescuers whose identity Hilde didn't know, and were whisked away.

It was a scene that was repeated two or three times a week. Every time she turned over a child, Hilde felt melancholy. *These children are being separated from their parents because of Hitler's sick plot to destroy the Jews,* she told herself. *I pray that the families who take in these children will be good to them.*

What Hilde and the other student nurses didn't know at the time was that they were part of a larger underground network that smuggled Westerbork-bound Jewish children into Christian homes. Two groups were formed by students at universities in Amsterdam and Utrecht.

A third group was founded by two Dutch Christians, Jaap Musch, a laboratory technician, and Joop Woortman, a cabdriver. While drinking coffee in a café in Amsterdam, they were discussing their outrage over the Nazis' deportation of the Jews. They had seen families herded into the Hollandse Schouwburg and knew that children were staying at the Crèche. So they decided to approach Mrs. Pimentel about rescuing the children, and she agreed to the plan. These three groups became known as the Anonymous Company or the Limited Group. It was so secret that even Hilde and her fellow student nurses didn't know its name.

As thousands of Jews were moved in and out of the theater, the families still believed that they were heading to work camps. They weren't so willing to give up their children. But rumors that later turned out to be true began surfacing that the Nazis were sending them to concentration camps and, ultimately, death.

That's why it was so hard for Hilde to see people she knew in the theater. Once, to her horror, she spotted her uncle and aunt, Paul and Jenny Cassel, and her twenty-two-year-old cousin, Vera, huddled in a corner.

"I can get you out of here," Hilde whispered to Vera.

"How?"

"I can get you a uniform just like mine," Hilde replied. "They'll think you're a nurse."

Vera shook her head. "My parents and I will be better off together. We're going to Westerbork. From there the Nazis will give us work in Germany. But if I sneak out and they catch me, we could all end up much worse. I can't ask you to take that risk, Hilde."

"I'm willing to do it. You'll be safe."

"Thanks anyway, Hilde. You'll see. It'll all work out for the best."

"If only I could believe that."

It was the last time Hilde saw her aunt, uncle, and cousin.

Despite the emotional moments of seeing friends and relatives deported and weeping parents saying a final good-bye to their children, Hilde continued to help smuggle toddlers out of the Crèche. But after eight months of rescue work, she was sidelined by diphtheria, a contagious disease that affected her breathing. She had to leave the Crèche and return home to her parents during her illness.

Late one night, violent banging on the apartment door woke her up. Hilde quickly slipped into her nurse's uniform and opened the door. Outside stood a Gestapo officer. "Get your things and come with us," the Nazi snapped. "You are to report for transport to a labor camp in Germany."

Hilde pointed to a sign on the door: QUARANTINE. DIPHTHERIA. "Do you see this? The illness is highly contagious and makes no distinction between Germans and Jews. It'll get you, too, the longer you are in contact with anyone in this apartment."

The officer spun on his heels and rushed down the two flights of stairs.

But the Germans came again and again, hammering on the door at night. Each time, Hilde, wearing her uniform, delivered her lecture on the illness, sending the soldiers fleeing. Hilde and her parents always got a chuckle out of the Nazis' reactions, but it was no joke.

"Eventually, the Germans will try to take you away, and then us," Hilde's father told her. "I'm not about to let that happen. We need to hide. I found a place for the three of us not far from here, but it was just bombed. I've found another safe house, a doctor's family, but they have room only for you."

"What will happen to you and Mama?" she asked.

"We will find something. Don't worry."

That night, Hilde ripped the Jewish star off

her sleeve and, escorted by a member of the underground, took a train to a small town two hours away, where she was dropped off at the family's house. After Hilde settled in, the mother took her aside and hissed, "I don't want you to have anything to do with my two children. You are here strictly as a maid."

"Fine," said Hilde. "I understand." But inside she was panicking. *If she acts this way toward me now, when she doesn't know me, I can't possibly trust her. What would happen if one day she was displeased with me? She'd betray me without a second thought. I can't stay here.*

Hilde was on the next train back to Amsterdam, alone and without papers or her yellow star. *This is crazy,* Hilde thought. *There are German soldiers all over the place. One could grab me at any second, but I don't know what else to do except go back home.*

She arrived in Amsterdam early in the morning. When she reached the front door, she recoiled in horror. The apartment was sealed off by a yellow rope. No one was inside. *The Nazis had been there again!*

Hilde ran over to her father's bookkeeper, Joop Kroeze, a Catholic, who lived about ten minutes away. "Do you know what's happened to my parents?" she asked frantically.

Mr. Kroeze put his hands on her shoulders and nodded slowly. "Your parents were taken away by the Nazis last night."

Hilde's knees started to buckle, but Mr. Kroeze caught her. She was still trying to process the news about her parents when he said, "I'm afraid this is the end, Hilde. The Nazis have made Amsterdam free of virtually all Jews, except for the ones in hiding, of course. And that's not all. I heard the Nazis have closed down the Crèche. The nurses and children are all gone."

Hilde slumped into a chair and wept. She felt sharp pangs in her heart as she thought about the Crèche, Mrs. Pimentel, Viri, Sieny, her fellow students, and of course, the children — all smiling and clapping as the nurses sang and played piano for them.

"I do have some good news for you, however," said Mr. Kroeze. "Your brother is alive! Jo is working for the Belgian underground, and I know a way for you to contact him. Meanwhile, you can stay here with my wife and me."

Before reuniting with Jo, Hilde felt a need to return to her family's home. With her next-door neighbors' permission, she slipped out their window, walked across the flat gravel roof, and broke into her apartment. She rummaged around until she found the one thing that was most important to her now, a priceless possession that she needed to keep with her until her dying breath.

She grabbed an album filled with photos of her mother, father, and brother, the student nurses, and some of the children she helped rescue at the Crèche.

Hilde joined Jo in the underground and aided in the rescue of downed British and Canadian pilots.

After the invasion of Normandy, in June 1944, Hilde and Jo joined the Civil Affairs Authority of the British army, riding in ambulances to the front lines in Germany to pick up wounded Allied soldiers.

While on one of these runs, Jo was taken prisoner by the Nazis. Hilde had no idea what had happened to him until her twentieth birthday, when she heard a familiar voice over the radio. The station had been allowing people to broadcast quick messages to loved ones. "Happy birthday, Hilde," she heard Jo say. "I'm okay." It was the best birthday present she ever received.

After the war, Jo moved to Switzerland where he became a businessman, got married, and had two daughters.

In 1945, Hilde joined the British Red Cross, which sent her to the liberated Bergen-Belsen concentration camp. There, thousands of Jews were dying from starvation, ty-

phus, and other diseases. Hilde soon learned that her parents had been at Bergen-Belsen, but when her father contracted tuberculosis, he and her mother were sent to Auschwitz, where they were murdered in the gas chamber.

While at Bergen-Belsen, Hilde started a child-care center. There she met a young doctor, Max Goldberg, and fell in love. They were married in 1947 and moved to Israel to help establish the new country. In 1950, the couple immigrated to the United States, where they settled in Teaneck, New Jersey, and raised three daughters, Rita, Susan, and Dorothy. Hilde and Max now have seven grandchildren.

Hilde, who devoted her life to education, never lost her love of children and never tired of teaching them the beautiful songs she learned as a student nurse in Amsterdam.

Thanks to people like Hilde, more than a thousand children were successfully smuggled out of the Crèche and into the loving homes of non-Jews. In virtually all cases, the children survived the war. Tragically, most of their parents didn't. Of the 110,000 Jews in Holland who were deported, only 5,000 returned.

Not a single child rescued by the Anonymous Company was captured by the Nazis, but two of its founders, Joop Woortman and Jaap Musch, were arrested. Musch was tortured and murdered, and Woortman was sent to Bergen-Belsen, where he perished. They and fourteen other members of the Anonymous Company were honored by Yad Vashem as Righteous Among the Nations.

At the end of the war, Hilde discovered that her fellow student nurse Sieny Kattenburg and nurse in charge, Viri Cohen, had survived.

It wasn't until two years later that Hilde learned the truth about the Frank family after reading a compelling book that became a worldwide best seller. The book revealed that her friend Margot Frank, Margot's sister, Anne, and their parents, Otto and Edith, had gone into hiding in Amsterdam but were eventually betrayed. All the Franks except Otto died in a concentration camp. After finding the diary of his younger daughter back in their former hiding place, Otto had it published in 1947. The book was Anne Frank's Diary of a Young Girl.

"I Am Safer in the Lion's Den"

Ferenc Schatz, Hungary, 1944–1945

As Allied planes overhead unloaded their cargo of death, eighteen-year-old Ferenc "Feri" Schatz lay still in a cornfield near Budapest, Hungary, and covered his ears, praying that none of the bombs would kill him. His body shook from the impact of each eardrum-shattering explosion — and from anxiety over what he was about to do.

He couldn't help but think of the irony of his dilemma. *I have survived so far, and now I'm going to be killed by bombs dropped by the Americans — the ones who are supposed to be saving people like me!* He tried to control his racing heart by taking deep breaths. *Don't panic. Just wait out the bombing raid, and then . . . you have to do it. You must escape today. It's your best chance.*

He didn't know how, but he hoped to find someone who would help him survive. Fate, however, had other plans, because soon Ferenc would be the one helping others survive.

Within minutes, the planes had emptied their load

and were heading back to their base. Ferenc and 200 other Jewish slave laborers were still alive after the latest bombing run. Like many times before, they had been repairing railroad tracks when they were forced to take cover during an air raid.

The whistle on their work locomotive gave three short toots. "All clear!" yelled the Nazi-supporting Hungarian guards. "Come out now and return to work!" The laborers dusted themselves off and emerged from the cornfield. But Ferenc didn't move. He stayed hidden, knowing the guards wouldn't discover him missing until evening, when they returned to their camp in Budapest and counted the workers.

Ferenc decided to stay put until work began on the tracks farther up the line. To remain calm, he closed his eyes and drifted back to his carefree childhood in Parkan, Czechoslovakia, where he romped and swam and rode his ponies. In his mind, he saw snapshots of his family in their large stone house: his kindhearted, wealthy parents, Edmund and Charlotte; his older brother, Béla; his older sister, Elizabeth, and her husband, also named Béla, and their infant daughter.

Ferenc pictured afternoons with his dad at the local coffeehouse, listening to grown-ups talk about politics; the spirited discussions at home around the dinner table; the steady stream of guests; the hungry Gypsies who were given food at the back door.

But the images in Ferenc's mind turned darker when he called up memories after the age of ten: the arrest, conviction, and six-month imprisonment of his father on a trumped-up spy charge; Hungary's takeover of the Czechoslovakian region where he lived; his sister, Elizabeth, her baby, and other local Jews being deported after the Nazi invasion; and his suffering in brutal forced labor camps. His brother and brother-in-law were in camps as well.

Ferenc thought about how the past few months on the railroad construction and repair corps had hardened him: the backbreaking work of shoveling hard clay out of coal cars; the senseless injuries caused when weakened workers dropped heavy rails on their legs; the cruel guards stealing his and fellow workers' meager belongings; the constant raids by Allied planes while repairing the same tracks they had already bombed.

After lying in the cornfield for an hour, Ferenc figured the guards were far enough away, judging from the sound of their voices. *There's no turning back,* he told himself. *It's time to escape.* He peeled off the outer layer of his clothes. Underneath was a much nicer set of clothes that gave the impression he was an ordinary citizen, not a slave laborer. He would no longer wear the yellow armband or the yellow Star of David that had been sewn on the front of his shirt. Out of his pocket he pulled a cap of the fascist youth organization Levente and put it on his head. *That should help avoid suspicion*, he thought. He had been hiding the clothes ever since a sympathetic farm family had given them to him a few weeks earlier.

On this chilly October morning in 1944, Ferenc walked out of the cornfield tired, hungry, and nervous. As he hiked along a country road toward a highway leading to Budapest, six miles away, he worried that he didn't have any identification papers. Every person was required to carry them, and he knew if he were caught without them he likely would be shot. He needed to avoid the Hungarian police, the German soldiers, and the vicious Arrow Cross, a militant fascist organization that needed no excuse to kill Jews, resistance fighters, or army deserters. Still, Ferenc felt he had a better chance of survival on the streets of Budapest than in a Nazi concentration camp, where workers were sent after repairing the railroad. He had three things in his favor: He spoke fluent Hungarian, he had some money, and he was familiar with the city.

When Ferenc reached the outskirts of Budapest, he bought a ticket on a tram and rode toward the center of the city. People were going about their business even though buildings had been scarred by bullet holes and charred from artillery shells and bombs.

Seeing a group of police up ahead, Ferenc jumped off the tram while it was still moving. This was where his escape plan ended. *Now what?* he wondered. *Where should I go? What should I do? I'd better act like I know where I'm going — and not make eye contact with anyone in uniform.* Feeling like a hunted wild animal in search of food and shelter, he strode down a crowded sidewalk when he unexpectedly heard his name.

"Feri! Feri! My God, I can't believe it's you!"

Ferenc froze at the sound of the familiar voice. As friendly arms wrapped around his slender body, Ferenc was stunned when he realized it was his sister's husband, Béla. Ferenc and his brother-in-law hadn't seen each other in more than a year, ever since Béla was drafted into the Hungarian Labor Service System and sent to the horrible copper mines in Bor, Serbia.

"You're alive!" shouted Ferenc. Suddenly aware that his excitement could draw attention, he lowered his voice, but he couldn't stem his elation. "It's unbelievable!"

"It's a miracle that we bumped into each other!" Béla said in a whisper.

For a brief moment, they silently stared at each other, their minds still reeling over their sheer luck, that despite having been in work camps hundreds of miles apart, they now had met by chance in the chaos of a war-torn city of more than one million people.

Ferenc broke the silence. "If I had jumped off the tram just thirty seconds later or earlier, I would've walked down a different street and we wouldn't have run into each other."

"Fate chose to smile on us for a change."

Then, in hushed tones, they told each other what had happened to them since they last saw each other. Like Ferenc, Béla had escaped from a slave labor camp. Now he was in Budapest, working for the underground.

"Have you heard from our family, from anyone back in Parkan?" Ferenc asked.

"Not a word," Béla replied. "It's too dangerous to get in touch with anybody because we're not sure who to trust there anymore. All the Jews in Parkan are gone." His eyes grew misty as he clutched Ferenc's arm. In a voice cracking with sorrow, he added, "I don't know what has happened to Elizabeth or our baby. I don't have a good feeling about their chances." Béla wiped his eyes and nose and then hugged Ferenc again. "Come, Feri," he said, putting on a brave smile. "I'll take you to a safe house so you can clean up, eat, rest, get some new clothes and a fake ID. Then you can decide what you want to do."

"What can I do?"

"Well, you can't just sit in a safe house all day. I want you to join me in the underground. You can help other Jewish refugees, supplying them with fake IDs and giving them money and finding them shelter. It's a full-time job. Of course, it's really dangerous work."

"It can't be any more dangerous than what I've been through already."

Ferenc was taken to one of the safe houses set up by Raoul Wallenberg, a Swedish diplomat whose mission was to save as many of Hungary's remaining 230,000 Jews as possible. Wallenberg had established hospitals, nurseries, soup kitchens, and safe houses throughout the city. Because Sweden was a neutral country during the war, he also was able to issue thousands of Swedish passports to Jews to protect them from deportation. More than 400,000 Jews had already been deported from Hungary.

Two days after Ferenc arrived in Budapest, he joined an underground Zionist youth organization dedicated to helping save Jews. The group had about thirty members, including some who grew up in or near Parkan and knew Ferenc. One of them was Vera Lefkowitz, a cute young woman with a rosy complexion and a winning smile. When they were younger, she and Ferenc often played together in the summer. He was always impressed with how strong a swimmer she was.

After they caught up on each other's lives and laughed about old childhood memories, Vera's mood changed. She glowered as she handed Ferenc a crumpled piece of paper and said, "Feri, look at the lies the Nazis are feeding to the people."

It was an official notice from the Nazi-backed Hungarian government. It read, "We warn the Hungarian Christian public that certain Jewish individuals have placed poisoned lump-sugar by house gates with which they want to endanger the life and health of Hungarian Christian children."

"The Nazis and fascists and the Hungarian government are making it harder and harder for Jews," Vera told Ferenc. "Everyone in Budapest is afraid. You must be very careful.

"In some ways it's more dangerous to be in the underground than in a concentration camp. Inside the camps, survival depends mostly on chance. But in the underground, you rely on your own wits, ingenuity, and instinct. You live in a sea of mostly hostile people, including informers, and you're hunted relentlessly by Nazis. Every decision you make can mean the difference between life and death for you and the Jews you're trying to save.

"This business can play havoc with your mind. I've heard stories of people living under an assumed name for months who couldn't cope with the tension and the pressure of working in the underground any longer. They made mistakes and ended up dead."

"Don't worry, Vera," said Ferenc. "I don't intend to make any mistakes. I'll be careful."

Béla arranged for Ferenc to get his first fake documents. "For your new identity, you should keep your first name and change your last name, but pick one that starts with the same letter," Béla told him.

"From now on, I'll be known as Ferenc Szabo."

"Good. You can keep the same month and day of your birth, but you'll have to make yourself a year younger because the Hungarian army is drafting men as young as eighteen. We'll make you seventeen. It's a good thing you're short and skinny because you can easily pass for seventeen. Now, what religion do you want to be?"

"Most everyone in Hungary is Catholic, but I don't know anything about their teachings or rituals, so if I'm stopped and questioned at a checkpoint . . ."

"Okay, we'll make you a member of the Evangelical Reformist Church. Few Nazis or fascists know anything about the religion. Next, we need to come up with a place where you were born. It should be somewhere that'd be difficult, if not impossible, for anyone to check."

"What about Siofok? I heard it's now occupied by the Russians. There's no way for the Nazis to verify my birth certificate there."

"Do you know anything about the town?"

"Yes, I had a cousin who lived there, and sometimes I went to his house on vacation."

"Perfect! Now you need to come up with a story about who you are so that you can use it whenever you're stopped by the police or the militia or the Nazis."

"How's this? I'm the son of a widower who's a superintendent at an apartment building in Siofok. I recently escaped from there when the Russians advanced toward the town. I made my way to Budapest, and I'm looking for work."

By the end of the day, Ferenc had an official paper with his new identity and a fake birth certificate issued by the church. He also carried a third document, complete with his photo, stating in French, German, and Hungarian that he was a part-time employee of the International Red Cross.

"It's only a matter of time before the Germans are defeated," Béla told Ferenc. "The Russians are battling their way toward Budapest, and the Nazis are getting desperate. Right now their main goal is to clear the city of all the Jews before the Russians come.

"That's why it's our job to supply other Jews with fake baptism papers and personal identification to show they're Christians and can't be taken away. We know the Nazi mind respects the authority behind official-looking documents, so we've created all kinds of formal papers, complete with numbers and seals. We need to get them into the hands of Jews in hiding.

"So here's your first assignment, Feri. A Jewish man has been hiding in the home of a Christian family for a few weeks, but they sent word to us that they can't keep him anymore. They're afraid that one of the neighbors suspects something. We have to help him before they put him out in the street."

After learning a few facts about the man, Ferenc filled out a fake identity card, then stepped on it so it was dirty and looked worn. He stuck the document under his shirt and walked to the house. "I have something for you," Ferenc said to the man in hiding. Handing him his identity card, Ferenc said, "You're now officially Josef Varga, a Hungarian from Debrecen who has fled from the Russians."

As tears of gratitude streamed down Josef's face, he told Ferenc, "You came from heaven. You're an angel." Before being escorted to a new safe house, Josef hugged Ferenc and members of the Christian family, who then kissed Ferenc and wished him well.

Over the next several months, similar scenes played out in Ferenc's secret life working for the underground. One day, it was an elderly man, the next, a young widow with a child or an escapee from a slave labor camp. Ferenc preferred to fill out the documents before he gave them to those in hiding. That way, in case he was stopped and searched, he could claim he had found the identity card and was returning it to its owner. If Ferenc was ever caught carrying blank documents, he would be arrested, tortured, and probably killed. But sometimes he had no choice but to take a blank document to a hidden Jew and fill it out there.

At checkpoints — it was virtually impossible to avoid them — Ferenc looked the police and soldiers in the eye and talked in a relaxed manner so they would drop any suspicions that he was Jewish. And that's when it dawned on him: *I am safer in the lion's den.*

So he left a safe house, freeing a bed for someone else, and walked right into the district headquarters of the enemy — the fascist organization Arrow Cross. He insisted on speaking with the commander, who agreed to see him.

"I'm a refugee from Siofok, and I have experience as a watchmaker," Ferenc lied. "I escaped from the Russians, and I seek your help. I need a place to stay and a job."

The commander looked at him and said, "You're not a Jew, are you?"

Ferenc laughed. "Would I be here if I was?"

The commander chuckled, too. "No Jew would be that brave or that stupid." Then he gave Ferenc temporary use of a room in a furnished luxury apartment taken over by the fascists. The commander also arranged for Ferenc to work at a factory that made timers for bombs used by the Luftwaffe, the German air force.

A few days later, Ferenc met Vera at an outdoor café. He couldn't stop smiling.

"Why are you in such a good mood?" she asked.

"Because you're looking at the newest member of the quality control inspection team at the Nazi bomb factory."

"Congratulations, Feri," she said, hoisting her cup of coffee.

"Yes, I'm the last one to look over the timers to decide if they're good enough."

Vera broke out in a mischievous grin. "Then that means . . ."

"Every chance I get, I can sabotage the timers. When no one is looking, I pull a wire so it won't work."

"Bravo, Feri!"

Because he was working for the German war machine, the job gave Ferenc cover to carry out his underground activities. Being in the factory also provided protection during the day from the frequent ID checks and raids by the fascist militia that roamed throughout the city.

After leaving the café, Ferenc went to check on a safe house that held about fifty Jewish orphans and children whose parents were in hiding. The kids, who were between the ages of five and fifteen, were being cared for by older students in a large villa in the swank Zuglo district of Budapest.

Ferenc was whistling while strolling down the sidewalk. As he approached the safe house, his whistle turned into a gasp. A group of five armed fascists were at the front door.

Oh, no. Not them. His first thought was to run, but he immediately discarded that notion. *I can't leave the children. Who knows what those thugs will do to them. I must find a way to protect the kids. Think fast! Think! Okay, I've got it. I'll act like I'm in authority. But if the fascists know I'm bluffing, they'll kill me. Well, here goes.*

He strode purposefully toward the leader of the group. "What are you doing here?" Ferenc demanded in a voice louder and an octave lower than normal.

"We're going to take the children to the ghetto."

If the children go to the ghetto, they'll be put on a transport to a concentration camp and never be seen again. I can't let that happen. "You can't take them," Ferenc declared.

"Why not?"

Ferenc pointed to a printed poster attached to the front door. "As you can see for yourself, this poster says this house is under the protection of the International Red Cross."

"So what?"

Ferenc pulled out his IRC document and held it in the face of the leader. "I'm a representative of the IRC, and I say the children are *not* to be taken anywhere."

"I am a member of Arrow Cross, and I say we can do whatever we want with these dirty Jews."

"Not here. Not now. I repeat, these children are under the protection of the IRC, and if you persist, I'll march straight to the Interior Ministry to lodge a formal protest and make your life miserable." *If you're going to get shot, it'll probably happen now. You might as well stand your ground. Don't give an inch.* "You have no papers giving you permission to take these children. You have no authorization."

The leader sneered at Ferenc and spit on the sidewalk. He spun around and told his group, "Let's go. We don't need to waste our time on little Jews when it's their parents we need to find." They stormed off.

Ferenc breathed deeply and plopped down on the front steps, too emotionally drained to remain on his feet. *I made them back down this time, but will I be so lucky next time?*

Danger was as much a part of his life as eating

and sleeping. Like any member of the underground, he accepted the hazards he faced. At any moment, at any checkpoint, at any street corner, he, or any of his colleagues, could be arrested.

"Feri," Béla said in a somber voice one wintry day, "an informant just told me that the Nazis arrested Vera."

"Oh, no," moaned Ferenc. "Not Vera." Ferenc's heart had been numbed by the years of Nazi cruelty and the ravages of war. It helped him cope whenever he faced tragedy. Still, this terrible news about a dear friend hurt badly, and he ached inside. "How did it happen?"

"She was stopped at a checkpoint, and she showed them her fake ID papers. They didn't believe her, and her story didn't check out. All we know is that they took her away."

"They'll torture her and then they'll kill her."

For the rest of the day and into a sleepless night, Ferenc couldn't get Vera out of his mind, fearing that she had died a horrible death. Making him feel even more distressed was knowing that she was caught doing the very same secret work that he was doing.

The next day, a middle-aged man knocked on Ferenc's apartment door and said he had news about Vera. Ferenc was suspicious, wondering if this was a trap — that while being tortured, Vera had given the Nazis his name. "I don't know who you're talking about it," Ferenc told him.

The man handed him a note: "Dear Feri, I was very sick, but I am feeling much better now thanks to my trusted friend. I need some medicine. Would you please bring it to me? You know what I need. Thanks. Vera." Ferenc studied the note. It was in Vera's handwriting.

"Who are you?" Ferenc demanded, still concerned this was a trick.

"I am Karoly Rozsa. I am a superintendent of an apartment building."

Ferenc became even more suspicious. By the very nature of their job, many such superintendents knew who was coming and going and made extra money acting as informants for the government. But many also aided the underground.

"Late last night," Rozsa continued, "a woman who was dripping wet knocked on my door and begged for help. I brought her inside and gave her a blanket and some food. She wrote this note and asked me to give it to you. She said you would pay me for my good deed."

Ferenc grunted. Bribery was a way of life in Budapest. It paid for silence, information, and cooperation. The problem was that if people could be bought by one side, they could be bought by the other side. Still, money was a powerful weapon that helped save countless Jews. Most of the cash the underground used for bribes came from American Jews who funneled funds through Switzerland.

Ferenc looked at Vera's note again and realized that she had written it in code in case it was intercepted. He reread the line "You know what I need." *Yes, I know exactly what she needs.*

"Sit down, Mr. Rozsa, and make yourself at home. I'll be back in a few minutes."

Ferenc rushed over to a nearby friend's place to gather a change of clothes for Vera, make a new fake ID, and pick up some money. When he returned, he told Mr. Rozsa, "Take me to her. Once I see her for myself, then I'll pay you for your good deed."

When they arrived at the superintendent's apartment, Ferenc and Vera embraced. "I thought for sure you were dead," he said.

Vera told him that after her arrest, she was tortured until she confessed that she was Jewish. "Late last night, they took me and about twenty other Jewish women down to the Danube," she said. "It was freezing cold outside. They ordered us to strip to our underwear and line up facing the river. Then they started shooting us so that we'd fall into the river and the swift current would carry away the bodies.

"You know what an excellent swimmer I am, Feri. So when the Nazis started shooting, I dove into the water and was swept downriver. It was so unbelievably cold I thought my heart would stop. I climbed out about a mile downstream. I knew I'd die if I stayed out in the cold much longer, so I went up to the first apartment house I saw and took my chances. I rang the doorbell of the superintendent and told him, 'If you help me, you'll be rewarded. If you don't help me, I will forever be on your conscience.' Thank goodness he agreed to help."

"I kept my side of the bargain," the superintendent reminded them.

"And now I'll keep mine," said Ferenc. He handed Mr. Rozsa enough money to equal the superintendent's salary for a month. "Thanks for your efforts. If you need help after the war, come see me."

Despite her harrowing escape, Vera continued to carry out her secret missions. So did Ferenc, who seemed to relish his perilous underground work, especially when he could do it right under the noses of the Nazis.

The Resistance needed places to meet and exchange information. One of the places they chose was Gundel's Restaurant, once the gathering place for the Hungarian upper class. Although the war had taken its toll on the restaurant, it was still one of the nicest in all of Budapest. And it was a favorite place to eat for the SS, Gestapo, and top-level officials of the Hungarian government. That's what made it the perfect meeting place for the underground. The enemy never imagined that members of the Jewish Resistance would plot against them while enjoying meals at a nearby table. Any onlooker would take Ferenc and his colleagues for typical Hungarian Christians — laughing, telling jokes, and having mindless chatter over a meal.

But during these gatherings, important information was exchanged through whispers and notes. Because Ferenc worked in a Nazi-supported factory and lived in an apartment building full of fascists, he'd tell his comrades about plans that he overheard of an impending raid or arrest. They'd warn one another of the latest government tactics, including lowering the age when boys could be drafted in the army.

In January 1945, the Soviet Union's advancing Red Army was tightening its noose around Budapest. In response, the Hungarian government tried to fill its ranks of soldiers with younger teenage boys.

"Bad news, Feri," said Béla. "They just announced that any boy sixteen and over has to report to military duty immediately. It's terrible. They get only a week or two of military training before they're sent to the front line and slaughtered by the Russians."

"I'll have to get new documents that say I'm fifteen."

"No one has any more blank documents. They're very hard to find."

"Then I'll have to find someone who can change the ones I have."

"Altering documents requires great care," said Béla. "I know a woman who has helped the underground before and has all the chemicals that can erase the old birth dates so you can change them. Her name is Klari Boros. She works in a private sanitarium."

The next day, Ferenc went to the sanitarium and met Klari. "It's so cold outside that it even freezes the breath of smokers," he said.

"What is even colder is the heart of a Nazi," replied Klari.

This was one of the code phrases that assured them they were both trusted members of the underground. It was always dangerous and nerve-racking to deal with an unknown person because he or she could easily turn out to be working for the enemy.

Klari took Ferenc's papers into a room. Using an eyedropper, she carefully squeezed a tiny amount of a chemical onto the year of the birth date, which had been written in black ink on all of his documents. It took a few minutes before the ink disappeared. "You'll have to wait about thirty minutes until the spots dry before I can write in a new year," Klari told Ferenc.

As they strolled in the corridor and made small talk, Ferenc noticed that the rooms were filled with patients of all ages. Doctors, nurses, and orderlies scurried about.

"Almost all the patients and staff are Jewish," Klari said.

"What about the ones who aren't?" Ferenc asked.

"We've bribed them into silence."

They were still exchanging chitchat when Ferenc suddenly felt antsy. This uneasy gut feeling grew stronger every second, until a voice in his head began shouting, *Get out! Get out now!* "I don't want to wait anymore," he told Klari. "Even if the documents aren't dry, I'll take them with me and fill in the dates later."

"If that's what you want, okay," she said. "But if you get stopped with those documents now . . ."

"I know. I'm dead."

A few minutes after Ferenc left, he heard the screeching of brakes. He turned around and saw that two army trucks had roared up to the front of the sanitarium. More than a dozen Arrow Cross fascists with machine guns jumped out and charged into the building. Ferenc wanted to run, but he didn't, fearing he'd raise suspicion. He walked away briskly, assuming the worst.

It wasn't until the next day that he learned in the newspaper of the horror that had unfolded there. Acting on an informant's tip, the death squad massacred all the patients in their beds and executed all the doctors and nurses on the spot. Ferenc felt sick to his stomach for the victims — and for realizing that he, too, would have been killed if he had stayed in the sanitarium a few minutes longer.

Despite the slaughter, Ferenc continued to live in the apartment owned by a woman whose son was a high-ranking leader of a fascist death squad. Ferenc felt relatively safe there. He figured that everyone else in the apartment — five anti-Semitic Nazi sympathizers — would never suspect that a Jew would dare live under the same roof. Besides, there would never be raids by Nazis hunting for Jews in such a building.

Living conditions in Budapest were becoming unbearable. The city was under daily siege from Allied bombs and Russian artillery. There were days when it was so intense that Ferenc couldn't get to the factory where he worked.

Whether or not he could get to work, Ferenc always returned to the apartment by five P.M., well before the citywide curfew of six P.M. The government warned that anyone who violated curfew would be shot on sight.

But one afternoon, Ferenc stayed out later than usual with friends and needed to hurry back to his apartment to beat the curfew. When he turned the corner of his street, he was startled by the chaos in front of him. People were sitting on the sidewalk, covered in blood and moaning in anguish. Smoke poured out of a gaping hole from his first-floor apartment. Rubble was strewn on the ground.

"What happened?" he asked a neighbor.

"Oh, my God, you're alive!" the neighbor shrieked.

"Why would you say that?"

"During the last air raid, a bomb struck the building and exploded," the neighbor replied. "Everyone in your apartment was killed."

"When did it happen?"

"About thirty minutes ago."

Ferenc shivered. *Thirty minutes ago? Had it been any*

other day, I would've been in the apartment. I would've died, too.

He entered what was left of the apartment to see if he could find his clothes, which he kept crammed in a cheap cardboard suitcase under his bed. Virtually everything in the room had been crushed or burned. He was about to turn away when he spotted his smashed suitcase. He shoved the rubble away and pulled it out. Incredibly, the clothes inside were squished but not damaged.

There was no time to dwell on this latest close call. *Move on,* he told himself, *and find another place.* As he walked away from the bombed-out apartment, Ferenc felt strangely confident. It was the second time he had beaten death. *The war is almost over. I'm going to survive. I know it.* He headed to a neighbor's basement, where he spent the night thinking about his upcoming missions for the underground. There was more work to do. More Jews to save.

When the war ended, Ferenc returned to his family's house in Parkan for a bittersweet reunion. His father, Edmund, had survived by hiding in the wine cellar of an employee, but his mother, Charlotte, refused to hide there. The Nazis took her away to a concentration camp, where she reportedly died from typhus just days after liberation. Ferenc's brother,

Béla, spent the last year of the war in a slave labor camp. He returned home more than a hundred pounds lighter. Ferenc's sister, Elizabeth, and her baby died in Auschwitz. Shortly after learning of his family's fate, Ferenc's brother-in-law, Béla, died of a heart attack.

The Schatzes' house in Parkan was not damaged during the war but had been looted of all its furniture. Luckily, friends had taken some of the family's possessions for safe-keeping and returned them. Ferenc and Edmund opened their home to returning Jewish survivors until they could get on with their lives.

Edmund continued as a businessman. Ferenc's brother, Béla, eventually immigrated to Israel, and so did Ferenc's friend Vera.

Ferenc worked as a translator for the Soviets and then became a newspaper correspondent in Prague, which today is the capital of the Czech Republic. He married Jaroslava "Jarka" Kremenakova, a Czech Catholic, who as a teenager was forced to work for the Germans.

When Czechoslovakia became a Communist country under Soviet domination, living conditions were nearly as repressive as they were under the Nazis, so Ferenc became a member of the anti-Communist underground. "Resistance to oppression had become a habit," he recalled years later. "We couldn't sit idly by. I was a journalist, and I used my ability to move around freely to arrange escapes for those in danger." But soon Ferenc and Jarka found themselves at risk when the secret police arrested and interrogated him. After his release, the underground suggested that the couple leave the country immediately.

In 1954, the Schatzes escaped with only the clothes on their backs and one small piece of hand luggage. For the next four years, Ferenc worked as a newspaper correspondent throughout Europe. In 1958, the couple immigrated to the United States, where Ferenc Americanized his name to Frank Shatz. He founded the Council on Foreign Policy in Lake Placid, New York, where he and Jarka founded their own highly successful leather company. Since 1980, he has been writing a weekly column on international affairs for the Virginia Gazette in Williamsburg, Virginia, where he and Jarka have a winter home.

The couple were instrumental in helping set up the world-class Reves Center for International Studies at the College of William & Mary in Williamsburg. Today, Frank gives lectures about the Holocaust to college students. "It is my feeling that I owe something to the world because I was saved so many times by miracles," he says today. "I am just attempting to pay that debt."

"How Can Those Collaborators Live with Themselves?"

LILIANE BELINNE, BELGIUM, 1942–1944

When Germany invaded Belgium in May 1940, thirteen-year-old Liliane Belinne, her mother, Germaine, her six-year-old brother, Francis, and several relatives fled in a truck from their hometown of La Louvière to the French port city of Dunkerque ninety miles away. Once there, they were hoping to board a ship to England.

Instead, they found themselves in even greater danger.

More than 300,000 British and French troops were trying to escape the advancing German army as Nazi dive-bombers screamed out of the sky, blasting roads, bridges, vehicles, and ships. At the harbor in Dunkerque, soldiers were jumping aboard boats of all kinds in a desperate attempt to sail across the English Channel to England. Thousands of Belgians, including the Belinnes, were trying to flee, too.

But as the civilians surged toward the boats,

British and French soldiers shouted, "Go back! We can't take you! Go back!"

Unable to stop the rushing mass of people, the soldiers resorted to shocking measures — they fired bursts of machine-gun rounds over the Belgians' heads.

"Mama, they're shooting at us!" Liliane screamed.

Yanking Francis by the hand, Germaine shouted, "Run, Liliane! Run into the fields!"

People scattered in all directions, some bolting toward their cars and trucks, others, like the Belinnes, dashing into the farm fields of tall grass away from the fierce combat. The air echoed with gunfire, explosions, and shrieks of terror.

Liliane, who in the panic was separated from her mother and brother, belly flopped onto the ground and curled up in a ball. *I don't want to die like this,* she thought.

She didn't move until the fighting stopped, hours later. Then, as she nervously stood up in the tall grass, Liliane heard a sound behind her that scared her so much, she fell to her knees and threw up. Slowly, she turned around. Staring back at her were the gentle brown eyes of a big, mooing cow.

Liliane couldn't help but giggle. *Bombs and guns were everywhere, but it's a cow that scared me the most!*

She got up and brushed herself off, then went looking for the rest of her family. She soon found them, unharmed. Luckily, the truck they came in wasn't damaged.

"The troops are never going to let us board a boat," Germaine said. "There are too many soldiers to move. They can't take civilians."

"Mother, why were the soldiers shooting at us? They're on *our* side."

"War does crazy things to people, Liliane. War can make friends turn against each other. It can make decent people do terrible things."

It was a lesson that Liliane would learn all too well.

After two exhausting weeks of dodging bombs, the family returned to La Louvière. But the town was not the same anymore. Nazis were every-where — on the streets, in the restaurants, in the stores — and they were mean and unpredictable. They often shouted orders to people that didn't seem to make sense.

One day, Francis had wandered across the street. Liliane started after him, but two Nazi soldiers pointed their rifles at her. "Halt!" one of them or-dered. "Don't cross the street."

Germaine stepped in front of Liliane and told the

soldiers, "My son is over there. I'm crossing the street to get him."

Liliane held her breath, fearing that the Nazis would shoot her mother at any moment. The soldiers kept their guns trained on Germaine as she went to her crying son, took him by the hand, and led him back. The soldiers lowered their weapons and walked away.

"Mother," Liliane said, "you took such a chance. They could've shot you."

"Nonsense," Germaine replied. "You have to stand up to them. They'll either back down or . . ."

"Or?"

"Or they'll shoot you. Liliane, I just couldn't leave Francis standing there or let you try to get him. What kind of mother would I be if I'd done that?"

"I don't know if you're very brave or very stubborn."

Germaine grinned. "Maybe a little of both."

Just like Daddy, thought Liliane. Her father, Charles, a tailor, had been drafted in the Belgian army but was captured by the Nazis and taken to a prisoner of war camp in Germany. She missed him badly, especially his easy manner, quick wit, and warm smile. It hurt her to think of him as a POW. She wondered if she'd ever see him again.

To make up for her father's absence, Liliane spent time with Léon Blanpain, a family friend who lived across the street. Léon was a wise, jolly man. He loved turtledoves, and had so many that their cage covered an entire wall in his house. He had a daughter named Lilly, but she had died from an illness, so Léon became a father figure to Liliane.

"I loathe the Nazis for what they're doing," he told her. "They're taking rights away from Jews and making their lives miserable. It's getting so bad that now we can be punished for being nice to Jews."

"I don't understand it," said Liliane. "Hating a person because of their religion is so wrong. Just because I'm Catholic doesn't mean I shouldn't have Jewish friends."

"The Nazis are bad people — and even worse are the collaborators," said Léon. "I no longer can trust people I've known here my whole life. They're spying on Jews or harassing them just to get a few extra rations of food and sugar from the Nazis. There are people in this very neighborhood who wouldn't think twice about tattling on you if you helped a Jew. By the way, I just heard the owners of the Jazz Café are suspected of being collaborators."

"Oh, no," Liliane groaned. "I love that place. My

best friend, Léonce Simonet, and I listen to the jazz sessions upstairs after school."

"Well, be careful what you say there — and in school. There are spies in the classroom, too."

"Are you still sneaking out at night and putting dead fish on collaborators' doorsteps?"

Léon smiled. "I don't know what you're talking about, but maybe you'd like to join me on a late night walk sometime."

A year after the occupation began, the Nazis announced that Jews were banned from attending public school. Liliane was angered when she heard some of her high school classmates cheering over the news.

She suspected that one of her classmates, Leni Moerman, was a collaborator. To test her suspicions, Liliane did something incredibly foolhardy. During lunch, she told Leni that two Allied pilots had been shot down over La Louvière. "I heard they parachuted and landed by the outskirts of town and were rescued by the underground before the Nazis could find them," said Liliane. "Isn't that great?" None of it was true. Liliane had made up the whole story to see Leni's reaction. Leni just shrugged her shoulders.

Maybe Leni isn't an informant after all, thought Liliane.

But that evening, just before dinner, the Gestapo came to Liliane's house and took her away for questioning. Her mother insisted on going with her, but when they arrived at Gestapo headquarters, Germaine was locked in a downstairs room while Liliane was taken upstairs and grilled about what she knew about the pilots.

Remembering how her mother had stood up to the German soldiers, Liliane looked her questioners in the eye and lied. "I've heard stories about how the underground saves pilots," she said.

"Tell me where you heard these stories," a Gestapo officer demanded.

"At a café."

"Which café?"

Think quickly, she told herself. *Whatever I say, it'll get the owners in trouble.* "The Jazz Café," she replied.

After Liliane and her mother were released, Germaine scolded her for "such a harebrained scheme."

Liliane promised never to pull a stunt like that again. "But at least I know who the informant is in my class."

At the end of summer 1941, Liliane and her family were overjoyed by the only happy surprise of the war — her father had been released from prison and had returned home.

Charles owned a tailor shop, which soon seemed busier than ever. Liliane noticed that customers would come in without dropping off or picking up clothes. Instead, they'd quietly talk about sabotaged Nazi supply lines, factories, strategic bridges, and roads, reports that never made it into the censored newspapers. Liliane soon figured it out. Her father was a member of the Belgian resistance movement.

Charles eventually enlisted Liliane's help with the cause. Her job was to make deliveries for the underground. On a regular basis, she would pack pistols, ammunition, or timing devices for bombs in her book bag and then coolly walk past German soldiers. She wasn't caught because the Nazis never suspected that a cute, perky teenager carrying a book bag would be working for the Resistance. Whenever she heard about a successful act of sabotage, Liliane felt a rush of pride.

The underground was also deeply involved in trying to help many of Belgium's 65,000 Jews who had lost their homes, livelihood, and rights.

"The cruelty and horror of the Nazis are concerns for all humanity, not just Jews," Germaine told Liliane.

Liliane knew that for her mother, the persecution of Jews was a very personal matter. Germaine had grown up with two orphaned Jewish boys from Poland, Charles and Simon Moncarz, who had been taken under her family's wing in 1918, after World War I. Germaine treated them as if they were her own brothers.

Liliane considered them her uncles, especially Charles, who was a *mensch*, Yiddish for nice guy. He was fond of children and would often come out of his furniture shop in the middle of the day to play hopscotch and other games with Liliane and her friends. Liliane enjoyed spending time with Charles, his wife, Blanche, and their daughter, Elsa, who was two years younger than she was.

The Moncarz brothers and their families managed to carry on with their lives as best they could. But in July 1942, Charles and his family were ordered to pack their belongings and report to the church square in La Louvière the next day. From there, they were to be taken by train to a camp in Malines, Belgium, before supposedly being sent to a work camp in Germany.

"Don't go," Germaine told them. "Gather the things you cherish most and hide in my home. If you go to a work camp, you'll never come back."

Charles, Blanche, and Elsa followed her advice. That night, they sneaked over to the Belinnes' three-story house, where they hid temporarily without Liliane's relatives and friends knowing anything about it.

Weeks later, as the roundup of Jews intensified, Simon Moncarz, his wife, Jeanne, and their daughter, Hetty, were given a work camp summons. They decided to hide at the Belinnes' house. But because Simon suspected he was being watched by informants, he felt the family should show up at the train station. So Germaine came up with a plan for their escape.

On the day Simon and his family were scheduled to leave, they went to the train station like other Jews who had been summoned. Liliane and her parents met them at the railroad platform, chatted for a few minutes, and pretended to say their good-byes while more than a dozen German soldiers stood guard.

"I have to go to the ladies' room," Liliane announced.

"I'll go with you," Germaine said.

They headed off to the ladies' room at the end of the platform. Jeanne and Hetty followed close behind. Then Charles went into the men's room and so did Simon. The Moncarz family left their luggage on the platform as if they were coming back to get it.

Inside the ladies' room, Jeanne and Hetty traded the colorful blouses they wore for the white ones worn by Liliane and Germaine. Meanwhile, in the men's room, Simon swapped his white shirt for Charles's blue one. Then, one by one, the Moncarz family slipped out an exit behind the restrooms to the street. Moments later, the Belinnes did the same thing.

It was scary for Liliane, who tried not to make eye contact with any soldier. She couldn't help but gaze sadly at the passengers waiting for the train to arrive. *I feel terrible for those Jews,* she thought. *They don't know what's in store for them.*

"You!" a soldier shouted to Liliane. "Stop! You're supposed to be on the train."

"No, I'm not," she declared in an assertive voice while battling to remain calm inside. She pulled out her identification papers. "See?"

He looked at her ID and then stared at her blouse. "I saw you on the platform with your luggage."

"No, you saw me say good-bye to some friends, that's all."

He glared at her. "If you know what's good for you, you won't have any Jewish friends. Now get out of here."

She nodded, took her identification papers out of his hand, and walked away. When she was out of his sight, she bolted for home and was happy to see that everyone else had made it there safely.

"Your plan to switch clothes worked great, Mother," she said. "But let's not try that trick again anytime soon. I came close to getting a one-way ticket to my doom."

Now the Belinnes were hiding six Jews.

Because food was rationed, it was hard to feed ten people in a house where only four were supposedly living.

"We have to do something," Germaine said at the dinner table. "If the Moncarzes stay here for any length of time, the Nazis will quickly figure out what we're up to. We have to find a way to get them fake documents and their own rations."

Germaine thought for days about how the Belinnes could continue hiding their Jewish friends. By now, the new school year had started for Liliane. As she was helping her mother prepare dinner, Liliane complained, "My first day back in school and already I have homework in geography class. I have to read about the Belgian Congo and —"

"That's it!" shouted Germaine, hugging her daughter. "You've helped me solve a big problem!"

"Mother, what are you talking about?"

"Aunt Rose, Uncle Yvon, and your cousins Christiane and Claudine." Germaine was referring to Liliane's relatives, the Neunezes. They were living in the central African country (known today as the Democratic Republic of the Congo) that was a colony of Belgium. "I'll tell the authorities here that my sister and her family have returned from the Congo."

"Oh, I get it," said Liliane. "Charles, Blanche, and Elsa are going to take on the identities of Aunt Rose, Uncle Yvon, and Christiane."

"We'll get papers and ration books for them," Germaine said. "Their documents will say they're Christians. That way, they'll be able to get jobs and an apartment. No one will know they're using someone else's names because it's almost impossible to check it out."

The next day, Germaine and Liliane strolled arm in arm over to city hall and spoke to Joseph Demotte, the mousy clerk behind the desk.

"I have good news, Mr. Demotte," said Germaine.

"My sister and her family are returning from the Congo. We'll need papers and ration books for them."

"How long have they been gone?" he asked.

"Two years."

"Do you know when they're arriving here?"

"Within a day," she said, still smiling.

Demotte cocked his head and, with an expression of suspicion, studied her face. He hesitated and then handed over the papers. "Have them fill out these forms."

"Thank you, Mr. Demotte," she said. "Good afternoon."

Germaine and Liliane went straight home. Because Liliane had excellent penmanship, she forged the signatures of her aunt, uncle, and cousin, copying them from letters that they had written.

With the forged documents, Charles Moncarz found work and an apartment for his family in another part of town where no one knew him.

A week later, Germaine went back to city hall to tell Mr. Demotte that three more relatives were arriving from the Congo. "Isn't that just wonderful?" she said.

"Why, yes, it is, Mrs. Belinne," he replied with a slight wink.

After Germaine got the forms, Liliane once again forged the signatures of real relatives who lived out of the country. These fake documents were for Simon and his family so they could move out of hiding with the Belinnes and start new lives pretending to be Belgian Christians.

But the Belinnes didn't stop there. Over the next two years, their home became a temporary hiding haven for twenty-three more Jews, all relatives of the Moncarz brothers. Although most of these refugees were originally from Poland, they spoke French well enough to pass as Belgian citizens in other parts of the country where most people spoke Flemish.

Each time a new family showed up at their doorstep, Germaine would go to city hall to get ration cards and another set of documents. "Good morning, Mrs. Belinne," Mr. Demotte would say when Germaine entered the office. "More relatives coming home from the Congo today?" With a faint smile on his lips, Mr. Demotte would hand over the papers that Liliane would later forge.

For Liliane and her younger brother, Francis, hiding Jews in their house meant keeping this secret from their closest friends because, if caught, the family faced deportation or even worse punishment.

Adding to the tension, an increasing number of citizens of La Louvière were collaborating with the Nazis.

"How can those collaborators live with themselves?" Liliane asked her mother.

"They're weak and they have no conscience," Germaine replied. "But they're very dangerous."

Although Francis was only eight years old, he was a bright boy who understood that he had to continue playing with friends whose parents were collaborators. Otherwise it might raise suspicions about the Belinnes.

Like Francis, Liliane was constantly aware that a slip of the tongue could be fatal for the entire family and the Jews they were helping. She continued to hang out with her friends, especially Léonce, although they didn't go to the Jazz Café anymore because the Gestapo had closed it down for "suspicious underground activity." Liliane and Léonce would spend hours gabbing about boys and movies and American film heartthrobs like Clark Gable and Cary Grant. Liliane knew better than to openly discuss her feelings about the Nazis and the Jews even though she was pretty confident Léonce would approve of the Belinnes' secret efforts. Still, there were times when Liliane would gaze at her friends and wonder, *Would they turn me in if they knew what my family and I are doing?*

One evening after Liliane had delivered a timing device for the underground, she bumped into Léon Blanpain, who, she had discovered, was a trusted member of the Resistance.

"Liliane, would you kindly keep me company on my evening walk?" he asked.

"Okay," she replied. "Where are we going?"

"Oh, just a little stroll, and maybe one brief stop."

Pointing to a paper bag that he was holding, she asked, "What's in there?"

Léon grinned and whispered, "A fish — one smelly, dead fish."

Liliane raised her eyebrows. "Oh, is this one of your 'gifts' for a collaborator?"

He nodded. "We're almost there. Just around the corner. You keep on walking while I leave this on their front doorstep. I'll catch up with you."

Moments later, Liliane stood in shock. Leon was sneaking up the walkway of Léonce Simonet's house. *This must be a mistake,* she told herself. *It can't be true. Not the Simonets.*

When Léon rejoined her after leaving the dead fish, Liliane said, "Léon, you're wrong about them.

The Simonets can't be collaborators. Léonce is my best friend."

"I don't know about your friend, but her parents are. Be very careful, Liliane. You can't trust anyone. Even best friends."

"I hate this war," Liliane said, tears welling in her eyes. "I hate the Nazis and what they've done to the Jews and how they've twisted the minds of good people into doing such bad things."

Léon put his arm around Liliane and said, "When this war is over, many Belgians will be ashamed of what they did to the Jews or what they didn't do to help them. Those who did nothing must live with their guilt. And those who helped the Nazis must face punishment. As for me, I don't want to live here anymore. When the war ends and the Germans are defeated, I plan to go to America and start a new life."

"I'd like to go there, too, and see Hollywood and meet that dreamy Clark Gable."

"Perhaps we can live across the street from each other in America."

"Yes, Léon, I'd like that."

Daydreams were a luxury for Liliane. The war and shortages of food and fuel made life hard for all the people of Belgium. Still, the Belinnes selflessly kept an eye on the Jewish families who lived nearby under their new Christian identities. Germaine and Liliane would bring them extra food, making sure their basic needs were being met, even as the Belinnes struggled to get by on their own meager rations.

One of the Jewish families had a girl the same age as Liliane. Her name was Reinette Konigsman, and she seldom went outside because she had an overpowering fear of Nazis. She was so petrified of them that she couldn't conceal her terror when she passed one in the street. Members of the SS and the Gestapo were specially trained to spot people whose fear could betray their identity as Jews.

Soon after she had arrived in La Louvière, Reinette was strolling down the street with Liliane when a German officer began walking toward them. Reinette whimpered, and the color drained from her cheeks.

When Liliane saw Reinette's face turn white, she said, "Stop shaking and act casual."

But the young woman trembled even more as the German came closer. When Reinette's knees started buckling, Liliane knew she had to act fast. "No matter what I do, just keep walking," Liliane whispered. Then Liliane stepped out ahead and strode up to the officer, a tall, handsome man not much older than she was.

"Excuse me, sir," Liliane said in a clear voice. "Can you tell me the time, please?"

Liliane moved over to his left side so he would have to turn his head away from Reinette, who was approaching him from the right.

The German stopped, looked at his watch, and said, "It's half past two."

Out of the corner of her eye, Liliane saw Reinette. *She's still pale and shaking. I wish she'd speed up a little. I've got to keep him from looking at her. I must keep his attention focused on me.* Liliane smiled in her most charming manner, leaned toward him, and asked, "So, where are you from?"

"Berlin," the young officer replied, smiling back.

Reinette was taking one faltering step after another. *Move faster, Reinette, and don't fall apart.* "I've never been to Berlin," Liliane told the officer. "What's it like?"

"It is a big city, very busy," he replied. "There are grand public buildings and museums, wonderful restaurants, and lively pubs."

"Oh, that sounds so exciting." *Reinette, keep moving. Keep yourself under control.*

"Yes, a pretty *fraülein* like you would love strolling

on Unter den Linden. It has some of the finest shops in all of Germany."

"Better than Brussels?" *Thank goodness, Reinette has passed him.*

"Yes, much better and very different," the officer said. "Perhaps we should talk more about Berlin at the café?"

"Oh, uh, what time did you say it was?"

"Only if you tell me your name."

"Liliane."

"It's two-thirty-two, Liliane," the German said.

"Oh, my, I'm late. I must go. Good-bye."

She hustled off until she caught up with Reinette, who had started to get the color back in her face. Once they were out of his sight, Liliane said, "Reinette, don't do that again. You'll give yourself away. You can't let the Nazis know that you're afraid."

Reinette tried, but she always looked frightened whenever she passed a Nazi. So Liliane often walked with her, distracting young soldiers by flirting with them.

In late 1942, Tova Luczka, the twenty-five-year-old niece of the Moncarz brothers, arrived in Brussels and sent word that she needed the Belinnes' help. Liliane's parents traveled to Brussels and brought Tova back, but it was obvious she couldn't live on her own in Belgium with a new identity like the Belinnes' other Jewish families. The only languages Tova could speak fluently were Polish and Yiddish. If she opened her mouth, it would be a dead giveaway that she wasn't a Belgian citizen.

"We'll never teach her enough French to pass for Belgian," Germaine said.

"Why does she have to speak at all?" asked Liliane.

Germaine clapped her hands. "You're absolutely right. She can pretend she's deaf and unable to speak."

It wasn't as easy as it seemed. Tova couldn't respond to any sound or to anyone, even a German soldier, calling out to her on the street. Liliane's father put Tova to work sewing in his shop, where she had strict orders not to speak. The same was true when the Belinnes had friends and relatives over, because no one else knew. Even Liliane's grandfather didn't know that Tova was acting the part of a deaf person who couldn't speak.

The only time that Tova could speak was when she was alone with the Belinnes in their home. She was free to talk and sing in the bedroom she shared with Liliane. Many nights, Liliane would fall asleep to the sound of Tova's voice, singing in Yiddish.

It was especially hard for Tova during air raids when Allied planes were bombing the Nazi-occupied town. She had to control herself all the time, making sure she didn't flinch even when the sirens wailed and explosions shook the ground. During the raids, Liliane's father stayed with Tova in the shop while everyone else scurried into the underground shelters.

Being forced into silence made Tova hysterical sometimes at night in her room. When Tova would sob, Liliane tried calming her by holding her and singing soothing songs. But as the war dragged on, it became hard even for Liliane to keep her composure, especially when the bombing raids became more frequent.

Liliane was devastated when she lost several school friends during an attack. They had been buried alive under the rubble after bombs from Allied planes accidentally hit the school. The students died before rescuers could dig them out.

While dealing with that heartache, Liliane suffered even deeper sorrow in the summer of 1944. She was outside in front of her house when two black cars pulled up. Liliane instinctively hid behind a tree. *Oh, my God, the Gestapo! They found out about us! Wait, they're not coming here. They're going to Léon's house.*

The officers burst into his home and dragged Léon out. As they stuffed him into a car, Liliane ran up to him. "Léon, what's happening?"

Although frightened, he flashed his trademark grin and said, "I guess they don't like fish." Before the officers slammed the car door, his expression grew somber and he yelled out, "Liliane, if I don't come back, you must go to America for me!"

"I promise," she said through her tears, but her quivering voice was too faint for him to hear as the car sped off.

A month later, in September, the postman, Rudy Michel, came to the Belinnes' door, and Liliane let him in. "I need to speak to your parents right away," he said abruptly.

The postman was a friend of Liliane's father and sympathetic to the Resistance. Whenever he saw a letter addressed to the Gestapo, he'd steam it open and read it. Often, the letter was from an informant reporting a neighbor for hiding or helping Jews. Rudy would then warn the neighbor.

"I intercepted a letter to the Gestapo and opened

it," he told the Belinnes. "It said that all of you have been helping Jews."

"Who betrayed us?" asked Liliane's father.

"It wasn't signed."

"I bet it's the same collaborator who turned in Léon," said Liliane.

"Maybe," Rudy said. "I destroyed the letter."

"Yes, but he'll just send another one," said Charles. "As soon as the letter reaches the Gestapo, police will come to arrest us and send us to a concentration camp."

"We must find a place to hide," Germaine said.

Late that night, Charles, Germaine, Liliane, Francis, and Tova rushed over to the home of Giuseppe Scapatori, an Italian diplomat who was an acquaintance of Charles's. Giuseppe led them up to a small attic. "You can stay here until the war is over," he told them. "It should be real soon. I've received reports that the Americans are close by."

Three days later, the Belinnes heard footsteps bounding up the stairs to the attic. The diplomat had always walked quietly to the attic, so Liliane held her breath, fearing that the Nazis had found their hiding place. The door was flung open.

It was Giuseppe. "The Americans are here!" he bellowed. "It's over!"

Liliane and her family raced down the steps and into the streets, where people were cheering and kissing one another. The Belinnes ran into some of their relatives and embraced them. Tova, who had not spoken in public for two years, was joyfully jabbering away.

When Liliane's grandfather heard Tova talk, his eyes grew big. "This girl could neither hear nor speak, and now look at her!" he shouted. "It's a miracle!"

Liliane and her family roared with laughter and then told him the truth about Tova.

The old man's face twisted into a scowl of hurt and anger. "Why did you lie to me all this time? I'm your flesh and blood."

But then Tova gave him a hug and said, "Don't be angry." Pointing to the Belinnes, she said, "Thanks to this brave family, twenty-nine Jews were saved from certain death. So you see, you still witnessed a miracle."

After Germany's defeat, 500,000 Belgians were investigated for collaboration with the Nazis. As a result, tens of thousands were jailed, fined, and lost their property. Three thousand were sentenced to death, although only 242 were ever executed.

Turned in by a collaborator, family friend Léon Blanpain was taken by the Gestapo to a concentration camp, where he was murdered just weeks before the war ended.

Liliane made good on her promise to Léon. In 1948, she and her immediate family moved to the United States and settled in New Jersey. Liliane married Hugh Gaffney, raised two children, and became a professor of linguistics at Fairleigh Dickinson University in Teaneck, New Jersey.

Francis became a test pilot and settled in Las Vegas, Nevada.

All of the Jews who spent the war pretending to be the Belinnes' relatives from the Congo survived and remained close friends of the family.

Liliane's father, Charles, died in 1965. Her mother, Germaine, who died in 2004 at the age of ninety-six, was honored by Yad Vashem as one of the Righteous Among the Nations.

"It's a Matter of Decency"

As a dozen frightened Jews huddled silently together in the hold of the old fishing boat, Preben Munch-Nielsen stood on the bow and scanned the choppy water for signs of Nazi patrol ships.

The fumes from the sputtering engine of his twenty-one-foot wooden vessel made him cough every time he undertook one of these secret voyages. They were heading across the Oresund, the waterway that separates Denmark from Sweden, a neutral country that was a safe haven for Jews fleeing from the Nazis. During the crossing on this particular night, clouds covered the moon and a sharp southerly wind caused the boat to pitch and roll. *This is good refugee weather*, he thought. *The Nazis will have a tough time finding us tonight.*

Preben checked on the passengers below. No one said anything. *That's good*, he thought. *The less talk, the better.* He didn't know any of their names. He didn't want to know them. It was safer that way because the less he knew, the less he could tell the Nazis if he was caught and tortured.

What fear Preben felt was overpowered by a sense of pride in a job for which he received something much greater than money — satisfaction that he was doing the right thing. He was working for one of the dozens of secret organizations of Danish citizens willing to risk their lives to help Denmark's 7,500 Jews escape the clutches of the Nazis.

The lanky blue-eyed teenager rubbed his hands through his wavy blond hair and gazed ahead at the Swedish coast, which twinkled like a string of white Christmas lights against the blackness of the night. *We're going to make it,* he told himself. *But what about the next trip? And the one after that? Will we get all the Jews across before the Nazis stop us?*

Except for the unexpected death of his mother, Preben had enjoyed a wonderful childhood in the quaint fishing village of Snekkersten, Denmark. He and his sister, Grethe, lived with their grandmother Augusta Munch-Nielsen in a large house while their father worked in Copenhagen. At the same time, Augusta also reared four of their cousins in a Lutheran household filled with love. For fun, Preben sailed during the summer, skated in winter, and hiked in the coastal woods. He did his chores at home without protest — although he never stopped complaining about weeding the garden.

Smart for his age, Preben attended the prestigious Metropolitan School in Copenhagen, thirty miles away. Every weekday morning, he'd ride his bicycle to the Snekkersten station and hop on the commuter train for the hour ride to his school.

Life was pleasant and uneventful — until the morning of April 9, 1940. When Preben awakened that day, the thirteen-year-old boy looked up at the sky with excitement, awe, and concern. Overhead droned wave after wave of German bombers, so many they seemed to blot out the sky. He didn't know what it meant, but his gut told him it wasn't good.

Still, he took the train to school that day. On board, he heard grown-ups chattering nervously about the growing war that Adolf Hitler had unleashed the previous year. Preben didn't know much about Hitler except that he was a feared, powerful man who had promised Denmark in writing that Germany would not invade the country.

When Preben got off the train in Copenhagen, leaflets that had been dropped from the planes fluttered in the breeze. He snatched one out of the air and read it. The message, printed in sloppy Danish, said that the Germans were occupying Denmark to "protect" the country from an Allied invasion. *That's a big lie,* he told himself. The notice also said that if the Danes tried to resist, there would be terrible consequences.

German soldiers in trucks, motorcycles, and on foot were pouring into the capital city. Already at every street corner stood armed Nazis. *This is bad, very bad,* Preben thought. *We had a treaty with Hitler and he broke it. What's going to happen to us?*

Like most everyone else, Preben, his classmates, and their teachers listened attentively when Denmark's King Christian X came on the radio. The king said that Denmark's small army was overwhelmingly outnumbered by Germany's. To avoid bloodshed, the king and the Danish government had reached a quick agreement with the Germans. Although Denmark was now under the control of the Nazis, the Danish government would carry on as before, including running the courts and overseeing the police. In exchange for not being attacked, Denmark's factories and farms would help supply the German war machine. Unlike in other countries under Nazi domination, Danish Jews were to be treated the same as all other Danish citizens.

Except for the presence of German soldiers, life for

Preben and most Danes went on as usual. But underneath the surface of Danish society bubbled a hatred and resentment of the Nazi occupation. Preben and most other citizens gave the German soldiers the cold shoulder and let their feelings be known in subtle ways. He and fellow students wore red, white, and blue caps, the colors of the British air force, the Nazis' main enemy. Workers in factories regularly went on strike and began sabotaging manufacturing equipment and railroad lines to hurt the Nazi cause. Danes often gathered in Tivoli, Copenhagen's colorful park, to sing patriotic Danish songs.

At the Metropolitan School, Preben, a polite, studious teen, was becoming increasingly vocal in his anger over the Nazi occupation.

"Our government collaborated with the Germans, and I don't like it," Preben told one of his instructors, Frode Jacobsen. "The Nazis control all the news and feed us lies, and our leaders do nothing. They're cowards and I feel ashamed. This is the first time in all our history we've lost our freedom."

"Freedom is something you don't think about until you lose it, and then you find out what it really means," said Jacobsen, a short man who spoke with strong hand gestures and a loud voice. He wasn't silent about his own disgust for the Nazis.

"Preben, if you feel ashamed to be a Dane, then it's time you do something about it. Stand up and show that you won't be beaten. The principles that the Nazis want us to follow are against everything that decent men have learned to love and believe in."

"But I'm just a kid. What can I do against the Nazis?"

"Wars are not always won with bullets and bombs. They are often won with heart, courage, and truth."

While walking toward the train station after school, Preben met Arne Sejr, a seventeen-year-old student at the University of Copenhagen. Arne was so outraged by the German occupation that he wrote his own "Ten Commandments to the Danes," which he had printed up in a leaflet. He handed a copy to Preben. The leaflet said:

1. *You must not go to work in Germany.*
2. *You shall do a bad job for the Germans.*
3. *You shall work slowly for the Germans.*
4. *You shall destroy important machines and tools.*
5. *You shall destroy everything that may be of benefit to the Germans.*
6. *You shall delay all transport.*
7. *You shall boycott German films and papers.*

8. *You must not shop at Nazi stores.*
9. *You shall treat traitors for what they are worth.*
10. *You shall protect anyone chased by the Germans.*

Join the struggle for the freedom of Denmark!

"This is great," Preben told Arne. "Everybody should have a copy of this."

"I'm angry that people are accepting this occupation," said Arne. "They act as if they don't care about the future. Well, the younger generation cares — and the future doesn't include the Germans. So if the grown-ups won't do something, we will!"

That's all Preben needed to hear. He joined Arne's new organization, the Student Information Service, which defied the Nazis by secretly publishing its own underground newspaper, the *Students' Service News*. Using the university's presses, students printed stories condemning the Nazis and circulated the illegal paper throughout the city.

Preben began distributing other underground publications that had sprouted up throughout Denmark as well, the most important of which was called *Information*. The stories in it came from professional journalists who used fake names to protect themselves and their jobs. Soon hundreds of thousands of copies were secretly hand-delivered to citizens.

It was dangerous for a delivery boy to carry too many papers, so dozens of illegal presses were set up in villages throughout the country. This way, Preben took a few copies of the underground papers from Copenhagen to Snekkersten and, using stencils and a print-rolling machine, made new copies to distribute throughout his village. He knew which adults despised the Nazi occupation — the vast majority — and which ones sided with the Germans.

After finishing his homework one spring night in 1942, Preben took his briefcase and rode his bicycle around the village, knocking on doors and delivering the latest edition of *Information*. He was about halfway through his route when a local police officer jumped out from the shadows and ordered him to halt.

Preben gulped. *Should I run off? No, I can't do that. I need to remain calm.* "Hello, Officer. What can I do for you?"

The officer, who Preben recognized as Thormod Larsen, ignored the question. "What's your name?"

"Preben Munch-Nielsen, sir."

"What are you doing out so late? Don't you have schoolwork?"

"I finished it. I was just visiting a friend and I'm heading home."

"I saw what you were doing."

"What do you mean, sir?"

"Let me see what's inside your briefcase."

Preben's stomach churned. *I'm trapped. He'll turn me in to the Nazis and they'll torture me.*

"I said, let me see what's inside."

Reluctantly, Preben handed over the briefcase. The officer pulled out one of the newspapers and, using a small flashlight, scanned the stories.

"You realize you can be arrested for having copies of an illegal newspaper and for distributing them," Larsen said.

I'm caught red-handed, thought Preben. *Well, if I'm going to be arrested, I might as well let him know how I feel.* "You can't believe anything the regular newspapers say because they only print what the Nazis want. So we need to spread the truth. Why should that be a crime?"

"Is the truth worth you risking the wrath of the Nazis?"

"Doing the right thing is always worth the risk, sir." *Well, that's it. Now he's going to arrest me.*

Larsen cracked a smile. The officer folded a copy of the paper, stuck it under his arm, and handed the briefcase — which still had the rest of the copies — back to Preben. "Your bicycle lamp," said Larsen. "Get it fixed." Then the officer stepped back into the shadows and walked away.

Preben was lucky this time because he knew there were policemen lurking around who reported to the Nazis. But he continued to deliver underground newspapers throughout Snekkersten over the next sixteen months. To Preben, it was vital that people learn about German concentration camps, arrests of Danish political prisoners, and the sabotage that freedom-loving Danes were committing against Nazis.

Fed up with the growing Danish Resistance, the German leaders declared a state of emergency on August 29, 1943, and ordered a crackdown that limited citizens' rights and privileges. When members of the Danish government resigned in protest, the Nazis took over running the country, restricting the Danes' freedoms and stripping the protection that the Jews had under Danish law.

A few weeks later, Preben was picking up copies of *Information* when Arne rushed up to him and ordered, "Throw those away!"

"Why?"

"We're coming out with a special edition to report

the big news. A high-ranking German official, one of the few who actually has a conscience, just tipped off our leaders that Hitler has ordered all Jews in Denmark to be rounded up and deported to concentration camps."

"When?" asked Preben.

"In a couple of weeks, on October first and second, which just happens to be the beginning of Rosh Hashanah, one of the holiest days in the Jewish calendar. Two ships are about to dock in Copenhagen, ready to take the Jews out of Denmark."

"But how do the Nazis know where the Jewish families live?"

"Remember all the synagogues that were broken into over the last few months? Well, the only things stolen were the registries that had the names and addresses of the members."

"The Jews better hide," said Preben.

"Or leave the country. The Swedish government learned of the Nazi plan and announced that Danish Jews will be allowed to enter Sweden — if they can get there. So we've got to let people know."

Preben scurried around Snekkersten, delivering the latest issues, all crammed with words that inspired people to act. Preben was especially moved by a statement that a former Danish government official wrote in the underground paper *Frit Danmark*: "We have helped the Jews and we shall go on helping them by all means at our disposal. If we desert them in their hour of misery, we desert our native country."

News about the impending raid spread like wildfire in Copenhagen, where most of the country's 7,500 Jews lived. Preben felt like most Danes: that persecution of Jews was against Danish culture and they wouldn't stand for it. He was proud that non-Jews from all walks of life and all parts of the country — clergymen, civil servants, doctors, store owners, farmers, fishermen, homemakers, and teachers — opened their hearts and homes to protect Jewish people. Christian churches hid Jewish holy documents and Jewish families. Thousands of Jews were allowed to hide in the homes of non-Jewish friends and strangers despite the danger to the hosts, and in hospitals, cottages, hotels, and even in the woods.

Two weeks before the planned raid, Officer Thormod Larsen came to Preben's door and asked, "Are you still delivering underground newspapers?"

At first, Preben wondered if the officer had switched sides and was working for the Nazis. But the manner in which he asked seemed to indicate otherwise. "Yes, I am."

"Good," said Larsen. "I have a job for you. There's a Jewish family who needs our help. Within an hour they'll arrive at the train station. Go there and meet them. Take them to Dr. Jorgen Gersfelt's home and stay there until you receive further orders."

"How will I know them?"

"You'll know them. Just look in their eyes."

Preben went to the station. He scanned the train platform as people streamed off. *There's no way I'll find them,* he thought. *I can't tell a Jew from a Catholic.* But then his eyes locked in on a family, each member carrying a suitcase. They looked wary and confused.

"Excuse me, may I help you?" Preben asked.

"Are you the one who'll take us to safety?" the man whispered.

"Yes."

Suddenly, the parents and children grabbed his hand and vigorously shook it. Preben smiled politely and escorted them to Dr. and Mrs. Gersfelt, who warmly greeted them. The doctor then took Preben aside and whispered, "Go to the Snekkersten Inn so you understand what's going on. Be here tomorrow evening at seven and take this family through the woods to the harbor in Espergaerde. Look for the boat owned by Erling Kiaer — you know, the local bookbinder. Make sure you get them on his boat between ten and eleven o'clock. You must be very careful. The Nazis are out looking for Jews. Their lives will be in your hands."

As a rush of excitement surged through his veins, Preben nodded. "Don't worry, Doctor. You can count on me."

"That's why we asked for your help," said Dr. Gersfelt.

Preben went immediately to the inn, a popular seaside hotel that had thirty-five rooms, a tavern, and a restaurant, and was sent to a crowded table in the corner. He recognized the owner, Henry Thomsen, and most of the others, local fishermen, shop owners, and fellow students.

Preben learned that the inn was more than just a busy hotel. It was also the center for an underground organization that would later be known as the Elsinore Sewing Club. The club, which had nothing to do with sewing, was made up of non-Jewish men and women who opposed the Nazis. Dozens of such secret groups had formed virtually overnight by recruiting people of all ages to help the Jews get to Sweden.

With Thomsen as its leader and soul of the Resistance, the Elsinore Sewing Club quickly grew to more than a hundred members, including Preben and Kiaer. Each person had a role to play in the planning, housing, and transporting of Jews out of the harbors of Snekkersten and the nearby villages of Elsinore and Espergaerde.

For several weeks now, the club founders had been meeting at the inn to make plans for smuggling Jews out of the country. Some Jews had already been taken to Sweden by rowboats, kayaks, sailboats, and dinghies belonging to local yachtsmen and summer residents. But then the Nazis banned leisure sailing, although it was still legal for fishing boats to sail because fishing was an important industry.

Thomsen, who now spent every waking moment running his secret organization, told his group, "We have about forty fishing boats in the Snekkersten area, so we're going to rely on them to get the Jews out. We've identified the trustworthy fishermen."

"The refugees will pay us for our expenses," said Kiaer. "But no one will be turned away if they can't afford to pay — not when lives are at stake."

"What about the guards at the harbor?" asked Preben.

"Most of the duty guards in the harbors and along the beaches are Danish, and they're prepared to support the Resistance," Thomsen replied. "They'll warn us of any pending raids and use delaying tactics when possible. If they see you, they'll turn their backs and say nothing."

When Preben arrived at Dr. Gersfelt's house the next evening, he noticed that every member of the refugee family appeared to be much stouter than he remembered. Then he realized why. Each person was wearing several layers of clothes because they weren't allowed to bring their suitcases.

Two of the family members were toddlers, so Dr. Gersfelt reluctantly gave them an injection that made them sleep. "I hate doing this, but we can't take a chance that they'll cry and alert the Nazis," he told their parents. "You'll have to carry them."

Turning to Preben, the doctor said, "Be on the lookout for Gestapo Juhl. He's determined to catch as many Jews as possible."

Preben knew all about Hans Juhl, a coldhearted Nazi officer. Fiercely hated by the entire community, Juhl would drive up and down the coastal roads in a gray car, urging citizens to report any

Jews in the area. Although he was short and had a baby face, Gestapo Juhl looked menacing because he carried a tommy gun, a handheld machine gun.

The family followed Preben as he crept through the woods. Not a word was spoken. When they reached Espergaerde, he spotted Erling Kiaer's moored boat, which had been taking up to a dozen refugees at a time across the Oresund. Pointing toward it, Preben whispered to the family, "Okay, all we have to do is walk across the road and onto that boat."

Just as they reached the dock, a police car pulled up. Officer Larsen jumped out and held up his hand. "Stop!" he ordered. "An informer alerted the Gestapo in Elsinore. They're coming here with more police. Go hide!" As Larsen hurried back in his car, he told Preben, "I must warn the others." Then he sped off.

"Follow me," Preben said to the family. They hustled into the woods and crawled under bushes. Peering through the branches, Preben saw Gestapo Juhl and his SS police swarming over the boat. Although Preben couldn't hear what was being said, he could tell that Gestapo Juhl was angry about not finding Jews on board. Throughout the search, Kiaer and his two crewmen kept smirking.

After the police left, Preben waited a few minutes before bringing the family on board. "Ah, Preben," Kiaer said with a wink, "you just missed a courtesy call from Gestapo Juhl."

Preben grinned and wished the family Godspeed before hopping onto the dock. As the boat pulled away, the head of the family said, "Thank you, Preben, for what you did for us. So we can keep you in our hearts, what's your last name?"

"It's not important. I'm a Dane — just like you."

In the days leading up to the Rosh Hashanah roundup, Jews arrived by train and car, lugging heavy suitcases and trunks and carrying small children. All the hotels and boardinghouses were fully booked, so beds were put up in their lobbies. Preben and ten other young men from the Elsinore Sewing Club were escorting dozens of small groups to boats like Kiaer's that were waiting with engines running. Other rescue organizations were secretly doing the same all along the east coast of Denmark.

Preben cheered out loud when he read in the latest issue of *Information* that the Germans' efforts to capture the country's Jews over the weekend had been a colossal failure. The Gestapo found fewer than 300, mostly those who were too old or sick to flee or had not received the warning. Of the thousands who made it safely to Sweden during the weekend, the Elsinore Sewing Club helped more than a thousand refugees. The Nazis had yet to figure out that so many civilians were rescuing Jews.

But Preben's joy quickly turned to deep concern. "The German patrols captured seven of our boats and arrested twelve men when they returned from Sweden yesterday," Thomsen told Preben and other club members. "They were taken to Horserod prison camp. They'll be tortured, those poor souls."

"Can we still run the other boats?" asked Kiaer, one of the lucky ones who hadn't been caught.

"No," replied Thomsen. "The Nazis are stationing new guards at the harbor. We need to know who they are before the transports can be resumed."

With fewer boats, longer waits, and a steady increase of refugees, Snekkersten was getting overcrowded and nerves were becoming frayed. To ease the strain, Preben and his comrades found Christian homes willing to hide Jews until the boat lift to Sweden resumed.

The day after the arrest of the dozen Snekkersten fishermen, Preben went to the train station to meet a Jewish family of five. When he arrived, he saw that they had brought four more refugees with them. He took all nine to the home of a Christian family, but it was obvious they couldn't all stay there, especially when it seemed it would be several days before they could sail. So Preben went to the neighbor's house and asked, "Can you take in four Jewish refugees for a couple of days?"

"Of course," said the woman. "They'd do the same for me."

Whenever he asked a non-Jewish family to harbor refugees, Preben was never refused. He wasn't surprised.

One day, his grandmother, who was suspicious because he was hardly ever home, confronted him. "You leave the house at all hours of the day and night," she told him. "Where do you go, and what are you doing?"

Preben had tried to keep his rescue work secret for her own safety. But finally, he revealed the truth. "I can't watch people in need and not do something," he added. "Somebody has to do these things. And, well, why shouldn't it be me? All of my friends are helping. We're in this together." He broke out in a sly grin and added, "It's also fun to aggravate the Germans." Then he stared at his grandmother's eyes, wondering how she would react.

She scrunched up her face in deep thought and

said, "I would be very, very disappointed in you if you didn't want to help."

The next day, Preben learned that Gestapo Juhl and his men had captured nineteen Jews in nearby Gilleleje Harbor. There was more bad news: A teenage crewman on a rescue boat was shot and killed by the Gestapo in Taarbaek Harbor. The next evening, Juhl and his men found eighty-five Jews hiding in a Gilleleje church attic. Twenty-two more Jews were captured during raids the same night, loaded into trucks, and taken to the Horserod prison camp.

At a daily briefing of the club, Thomsen told the members, "The Gestapo is tightening its grip over the fishing fleet. They're using informants to infiltrate the transport groups."

"We have ways of dealing with them," a member of the Resistance whispered to Preben. "Mrs. Sorensen, who lives up the road, is one we suspect of being a Nazi sympathizer. We sent her a funeral wreath a couple of days ago and followed it up yesterday with a card that had a black cross on it. She got the message."

Thomsen reported that sections of the Danish coast were guarded by German soldiers who had taken over private beachfront houses. The German navy also brought in faster and more maneuverable patrol boats that could outrun any of the Snekkersten fishing boats. "They can't guard the entire coast," he said. "We'll stay out of the harbor and load the refugees at night from open beaches and coves."

Night and day at the train station, Preben would go up to people who looked lost and scared and tell them, "I know where you'll be out of harm's way." He'd take them to a safe house and say, "Wait here until you hear from one of us when it's time to leave. Remember, you didn't walk here with anyone, and you don't know who I am."

Preben also went looking for refugees who were staying in the woods. Having spent so much time playing there when he was younger, he knew every good hiding spot. The refugees were often so frightened of being captured that it sometimes took Preben a couple of days to gain their trust.

When it was time, usually late at night, he took the refugees through backyards and gardens. He knew which yards to avoid because of barking dogs and which dogs stayed quiet when bribed with a treat from him. Preben led the families to a pre-arranged spot on a deserted part of the beach, signaled their arrival with his flashlight, and waited for Kiaer's boat.

The refugees sat there nervously, seeing the lights of Sweden across the Oresund. Freedom was so close, and the future so uncertain. Soon Kiaer flashed a signal that it was okay to come aboard. Then the families jumped into the ice-cold water, which was three or four feet deep, and waded out to the boat, where crewmen pulled them aboard.

Eventually, Preben helped out on Kiaer's boat, making two or three crossings a night. He escorted refugees and also an increasing number of resistance fighters who had been identified by informants and were wanted by the Gestapo.

The voyage across the Oresund took anywhere from forty-five minutes to two hours, depending on the weather and the number of German patrol boats to avoid. To cut the length of the trips in half, Swedish fishing boats often met Danish fishing boats in the middle of the Oresund and took the refugees the rest of the way.

But then one of the Danish fishing boats returned to Snekkersten Harbor and was boarded by guards who discovered the nets were dry. The Nazis seized the boat, knowing it had been used to ferry refugees. The Elsinore Sewing Club came up with a new plan. During the transfer of the refugees, the Danish fishermen would exchange their dry nets for fresh fish and wet nets from the Swedes. That way, if the Nazis stopped them, the Danes could claim they were just fishing.

On one of the crossings, Preben escorted a family headed by a cantor of a synagogue in Copenhagen. (A cantor sings religious songs and leads the congregation in prayer.)

"How do you know the German patrol boats won't find us?" the cantor's wife asked Preben.

"We take advantage of the Germans' punctuality," he replied. "You can always be sure the patrol boats will cruise by here at ten P.M. They won't be back at this spot for another four hours."

Preben's face turned grim after he ushered the family to the bow and covered them with the smelly fishing nets. One of the older children, his voice breaking, said to the others, "What have we ever done to deserve this?"

These poor devils, Preben thought. *The boy is right. What did they ever do except to be born Jewish?*

The crossing went just the way Preben liked it — uneventfully. When the boat neared the Swedish coast, he lifted the nets and found many of the refugees seasick and tired. "You can come out now," he told them. "It's safe."

The cantor emerged from the cramped hold and

gulped in a lungful of the fresh sea breeze. "I had no doubt that we'd make it," he told Preben. "All the Jews of Denmark will make it across safely."

"What makes you say that?"

"We Jews were given the warning to leave before the Nazis arrived. People of all faiths gave us sanctuary. And out of nowhere came this fleet of boats to rescue us. To me, this a clear sign — there will be no Holocaust in Denmark."

In a matter of weeks, the Danish people helped more than 7,000 Danish Jews flee to Sweden. The Nazis captured fewer than 500 Jews in Denmark and shipped them to Theresienstadt, a concentration camp in Czechoslovakia. The Danish Jews were given special treatment and weren't murdered. Most of them survived because the Nazis allowed the Danish citizens to send more than 700 packages of clothing, food, and vitamins for the prisoners to use in the camp.

In other Nazi-occupied countries, the Germans were able to deport and kill the Jews. But in Denmark, ninety-nine percent of the Jewish population survived the war years.

Even after there were no more refugees, Preben continued to work for the Elsinore Sewing Club as a crewman on a boat that transported downed Allied pilots and resistance fighters who were escaping from the Gestapo. The boat also brought mail, intelligence documents, and underground newspapers to Sweden and returned with weapons for the Resistance and mail from exiled Danes.

Preben himself became a refugee when, after a trip to Sweden, he was warned that it was unsafe for him return to Denmark. The Nazis had learned from a traitor that Preben was working for the underground. Fortunately, Preben had relatives in Sweden, so he stayed with them while he finished his senior year of high school. Then he joined the Danish Brigade, a military unit trained in Sweden for a possible attack against the Nazis in Denmark.

Most of the members of the Elsinore Sewing Club escaped to Sweden or were arrested. Others paid a steeper price.

While loading up refugees aboard Erling Kiaer's boat on January 20, 1944, Officer Thormod Larsen was shot and seriously wounded by the Gestapo. But friendly police managed to take him to a hospital, where he eventually recovered.

Rather than sit out the rest of the war, Kiaer resumed the increasingly dangerous transports. After his 142nd illegal crossing, the Nazis captured him on May 11, 1944. He was tortured and imprisoned for nearly a year before his release.

On August 9, 1944, the Gestapo, alerted by an informer, arrested Henry Thomsen, the leader of Snekkersten's rescue operation. He was tortured and thrown in a prison camp. On Christmas Eve of that year, his family received a letter from the camp commandant saying that Thomsen had died of pneumonia. A monument in his honor now stands in Snekkersten as a reminder of his courage and dedication.

After Germany surrendered on May 5, 1945, Dr. Jorgen Gersfelt continued his medical practice. Frode Jacobsen, one of Preben's influential high school instructors and a leader in the resistance movement, became a member of Denmark's parliament.

Preben returned home to Denmark and embarked on a career as a salesman before becoming a successful business-man in Copenhagen. He had six children and nine grand-children from two marriages.

In the early 1990s, Preben helped arrange for Kiaer's boat to be sent to the United States Holocaust Memorial Museum in Washington, D.C., where it is on permanent display. (You can see a photo of the boat online by going to **www.ushmm.org/outreach/89222-1.htm**). It's esti-mated that during the war, the boat carried 1,400 refugees to safety in Sweden.

Preben died in 2002 in Denmark. Before his death, he was interviewed twice by oral historians from the Holocaust Museum. The transcripts of those interviews formed the ba-sis for this story. "You can't turn your back on people who need your help," Preben once said. "It's a matter of decency."